21.47

BASIC numerical mathematics

D0782720

To

Moya and Chad

BASIC numerical mathematics

J C Mason MA, D Phil, FIMA

Principal Lecturer
Department of Mathematics and Ballistics
Royal Military College of Science, Shrivenham, England

Butterworths
London . Boston . Durban . Singapore . Sydney . Toronto . Wellington

First published 1983
Reprinted 1985

© Butterworth & Co (Publishers) Ltd, 1983

British Library Cataloguing in Publication Data

Mason, J. C.
BASIC numerical mathematics.
1. Basic (Computer program language)   2. Engineering
mathematics—Computer programs
I. Title
510′.28′542   TA330

ISBN 0-408-01137-8

Typeset by Phoenix Photosetting, Chatham, Kent
Printed and bound in Great Britain by Whitstable Litho Ltd., Whitstable, Kent.

Preface

This book has two broad aims, as its title suggests: to introduce the reader to numerical mathematics, and to do so in the context of BASIC language programming. It is thus hoped to meet the needs of a wide range of engineers, mathematicians, and scientists who wish to solve practical problems on a computer.

More specifically, the book is one of a series geared to the requirements of undergraduate engineers, both in its choice of topics and in its style of presentation. In this context it has two principal tasks: to present BASIC numerical mathematics for its intrinsic value to engineers, and to provide a foundation for applications of numerical mathematics in other books of the BASIC series.

In particular the book aims to cover to a reasonable depth a selection of the most fundamental topics, namely nonlinear equations, finite differences, interpolation, differentiation and integration, as well as a variety of elementary mathematical calculations. Books on further numerical topics will appear later in the BASIC series, including a text on BASIC Matrix Methods, covering direct and indirect methods for simultaneous linear equations and applications to data fitting and function approximation.

Although it is primarily intended as an introductory text for first and second year undergraduates, the book would also serve as a reference book for advanced undergraduates, and its more elementary sections could be understood by good mathematics and science students in schools.

The book contains not only a large number of well-documented BASIC programs for executing a number of fundamental mathematical methods required by engineers, but also a fairly detailed discussion of the mathematical principles behind these methods. As a textbook it is tailor-made for a course in which numerical mathematics and computing are 'integrated', but it could also provide a means of spicing up a numerical mathematics course by adding optional computer exercises or of strengthening an engineering problems course by offering not only 'package programs' but also the mathematical foundations underlying them.

In writing the computer programs for this book certain decisions had to be made. In particular, BASIC was chosen as the programming language for the book, indeed for the whole series of books, because it is a simple and convenient language which is justifiably popular amongst engineers and widely available on minicomputers. The design of the BASIC language makes it possible to write programs, test them, modify them, and run them with very great ease. Readers should therefore be able to use and modify the programs in the book for their own use without difficulty.

However, one notable drawback of BASIC lies in its poor subroutine and subprogram facilities; indeed it is not normally possible to call upon one program within another program. This and other drawbacks are pointed out in the book as they arise. Although subprogram facilities can generally be dispensed with at the elementary level of this book, readers would find such facilities helpful if they wished to develop programs or use them within their own programs. In time such facilities may well become available in BASIC on larger computer systems.

In order to promote better understanding, individual instructions in our BASIC programs have wherever possible been written to resemble corresponding mathematical equations, occasionally at the expense of a little efficiency. The resemblance becomes clearer if the reader erases all REM statements, which are included only for explanatory purposes.

If readers wish to look up programs in the book, they will find them within the body of the text rather than before or after the relevant theory. However, complete lists of programs with titles and page references may be found in the Contents List. Programs are generally preceded by Algorithms (with the same numbering) which detail the logical steps to be carried out, and followed by Sample Runs which demonstrate the programs in action, and by Program Notes which provide necessary additional information and advice.

So as to make the programs easy to use and attractive for demonstration and teaching purposes we have designed them to be 'interactive'. Following the keyboard instruction RUN, the user is asked for all relevant data, and then all input and output takes place at the keyboard. However, this also means that, if typed output is to be taken away by the user, the keyboard must be equipped with a 'hard-copy' facility. Readers who prefer to use 'batch-mode' programs, which include all their own data, may easily modify the programs by using appropriate READ and DATA statements in place of INPUT statements (see Programs 1A and 1B where such modifications are made).

As far as the mathematics in the book is concerned, we have tried to strike an appropriate balance between numerical methods and numerical analysis. It is clearly essential for engineers to have an armoury of methods at their disposal. However, they also need to know enough numerical analysis to be able to assess the relative merits of alternative methods and to understand the errors that all methods necessarily produce.

We have also tried to whet the reader's appetite in all the problem areas covered, even though in some cases the shortness of the book and the assumed inexperience of the reader has prevented us from making use of the 'best' methods available. On balance we believe that readers are better off with an imperfect method, provided that they are made aware of its limitations, than with no method at all.

A large number of problems are posed at the ends of chapters, covering both mathematical and computational aspects. Many of the questions are designed to help readers understand and use the theory and programs in the book. However, several questions are also given which aim to increase the reader's mathematical knowledge and put new perspectives on the theory, and several opportunities are given for readers to extend and develop programs to solve new problems.

It remains for us make some specific remarks about the contents. The book starts with three introductory chapters. Chapter 1 provides a brief but reasonably thorough description of BASIC, sufficient to understand and code the programs in the book. Chapter 2 gives an overall view of numerical mathematics, and discusses with simple examples all the factors which need to be taken into account in applying a numerical method to solve a mathematical problem. While Chapter 3 develops BASIC programs to perform a set of elementary mathematical calculations, several of which will be familiar to the reader from school mathematics (e.g. the solution of quadratic equations) and a number of which are used to advantage within programs in subsequent chapters.

Chapter 4 then proceeds to a thorough discussion of nonlinear algebraic equations including the bisection method, fixed point iteration and Newton's method, but with no treatment of complex roots. Finally Chapter 5 is concerned with the processing of tables of data in order to derive information from them, including the interpolation of values between tabulated values, the evaluation of derivatives (i.e. gradients), and the calculation of integrals (i.e. areas under the graph). This chapter includes a comprehensive introduction to finite differences, which are the principal tool in the analysis.

Although the book is primarily intended for undergraduate use, we suggest that introductory numerical mathematics/computing courses in schools might be based on Chapters 1 to 3, together with judiciously chosen sections of Chapters 4 and 5 (centering perhaps around the bisection and Newton methods, the Lagrange and Newton interpolation formulae, and the trapezium and Simpson integration rules).

We are grateful to colleagues at the Royal Military College of Science at Shrivenham for helping with this book in a variety of ways.

In particular we are indebted to Mrs Jan Price for preparing the manuscript with astonishing speed and precision, and to Mr D. C. Stocks, Dr M. J. Iremonger, and Mr P. D. Smith, for reading, checking or criticizing various parts of it.

J. C. M.

Contents

Chapter 1

Introduction to BASIC

"In a few minutes a computer can make a mistake so great that it would take many men many months to equal it", according to Merle L. Meacham. Nevertheless, when such mistakes can be avoided, the computer can be an invaluable tool in the solution of mathematical problems. In this book we must therefore strive not only to understand numerical mathematics but also to write correct BASIC computer programs.

1.1 Computer programs and programming languages

A computer program is a set of instructions which a computer is able to interpret and execute. These instructions are designed to perform a particular task, in our case the numerical solution of a mathematical problem. In order that the instructions may be recognised, they must be written in a standard programming language (such as BASIC, FORTRAN, ALGOL, PASCAL, COBOL, etc) for which an 'interpreter' (or 'compiler') is available on the computer. The interpreter transforms each instruction in the programming language into a set of fundamental instructions in a 'machine language' instantly recognisable to the computer. The programming language is designed to be convenient and practicable for the user, and BASIC is one such programming language.

1.2 The BASIC approach

All of the programs in this book are written in BASIC. The name BASIC is an acronym for Beginner's All-purpose Symbolic Instruction Code, and was developed at Dartmouth College USA as a general-purpose language. The main advantages of BASIC are that it is easy to learn, convenient to use, and particularly well suited to 'conversational' programming in which the user interacts with the computer throughout the running of the program.

The simple version of BASIC used in this book has a number of disadvantages, and these mainly concern its lack of structure in

1

comparison with languages like FORTRAN or PASCAL. For example it is not usual in BASIC to distinguish between integers and other numbers, to have variables of double length (for more accurate calculations), or to use one program as a subroutine or subprogram for another program. Moreover BASIC has a particular disadvantage in numerical analysis, which relates to its apparently commendable feature of rounding to integer values any numbers that are very close to integers. This makes it difficult to test the conditioning of any problem that has integer data, and inadvisable to use integer data as test data in gauging the rounding error in any program. However, these disadvantages are not too important a consideration for elementary programs such as those given in the following chapters.

This book is not intended as an instruction manual in BASIC. For that purpose the reader is referred to References 1–3 at the end of the Chapter or to one of many similar works. One of our aims, however, is to help the student learn BASIC by applying it to solve mathematical problems, especially those that occur in science and engineering. This aim can be met by the reader if he studies and tests the programs in the book, and also tries to write his own programs based on some of the problems given at the ends of the chapters. Although the book does not give every detail of the grammar of BASIC, a description of the main features of BASIC is given below.

1.3 The elements of BASIC

1.3.1 *Program structure and sequencing*

A BASIC program is a sequence of statements which define a procedure for the computer to follow (rather like a cooking recipe for a chef to follow). As it follows this procedure, the computer allocates values to each of the variables encountered and changes them where instructed. Statements used in the program are of a number of types, which will be discussed in more detail in following sections. They include REM statements (for making program notes), DIM statements (for allocating subscripted variables), INPUT or READ statements (for defining data), assignment statements (for doing mathematics), conditional statements (for controlling the action of the program) and PRINT statements (for printing out results).

Every statement must be preceded by a line number. On running the program, all statements are executed in the sequence that corresponds to these line numbers. For example, the program

100 X = 1	is executed as	100 X = 1
400 GO TO 200		200 X = X + 1
300 PRINT X		300 PRINT X
200 X = X + 1		400 GO TO 200

The use of numbering greatly simplifies correcting and editing (see Section 1.5).

1.3.2 *Mathematical expressions*

In mathematics it is necessary to evaluate expressions which involve numerical constants, variables (e.g. x), and functions (e.g. sin). All constants are treated identically in BASIC, whether they are integer (e.g. 36) or real (e.g. 36.1). They may be entered in either fixed point form (e.g. 36.1) or floating point form (e.g. 0.361E2), although the computer prints out numbers in fixed point form unless they are small or large. The constant π is often available by typing PI or the π key, but for clarity the numerical value (3.14159265 . . .) will be used in this book unless otherwise stated.

Variables which fulfil the role of letters in algebra, may be named by any one of the letters A to Z, or by any letter followed by a digit (e.g. A3, P7, etc). Each variable is allocated a location in the computer memory, and it takes the numerical value recorded in that location. This numerical value is substituted for the corresponding variable whenever that variable occurs in an expression, and so it is important to ensure that the correct value is given to a variable initially.

The function square root may be evaluated via the built-in computer function SQR, $\sqrt{x}$ being replaced by SQR(X). The argument in brackets (X) may be any number, variable, or mathematical expression. Other built-in functions include SIN(X), COS(X), LOG(X), EXP(X), ABS(X), and INT(X) which represent, respectively, $\sin x$, $\cos x$, $\ln x$ (i.e. $\log_e x$), e^x, $|x|$, and the integer part of x. For trigonometric functions (SIN, etc) the argument is assumed to be measured in radians.

Mathematical expressions are formed from constants, variables and functions by inserting arithmetic operations such as plus, times, etc. These operations have a hierarchy, which determines the order in which they are performed by the computer, and it is as follows:

to the power of ($^$)
multiply (*) and divide ($/$)
add ($+$) and subtract ($-$).

If two or more operations have the same hierarchy, then the computer works from left to right. Brackets always take precedence and should be used to provide clarity and avoid ambiguity. The first left bracket is paired with the last right bracket, and so on. Hence

$$\frac{a + b}{3c}$$

becomes either

$$(A+B)/(3^*C) \quad \text{or} \quad (A+B)/3/C.$$

Some examples of correct and incorrect BASIC expressions are as follows:

Mathematical expression	Correct BASIC	Incorrect BASIC
$x \sin x$	X * SIN(X)	X SIN(X)
$\dfrac{1 - r^n}{1 - r}$	$(1-R\char`\^N)/(1-R)$	$1-R\char`\^N/1-R$
$\ln(1 + \sqrt{x})$	LOG (1 + SQR(X))	LOG (1 + SQR(X)
$\left\lvert \dfrac{1 + \sin x}{x} \right\rvert$	ABS((1 + SIN(X))/X)	ABS (1 + SIN(X))/X

1.3.3 *Assignment statements*

An assignment statement takes the form

line number [LET] variable = mathematical expression

The word LET here is usually optional, and will be omitted throughout this book. Square brackets are used in this chapter to indicate optional items. For example a root of a quadratic equation

$$x_1 = (-b + \sqrt{b^2 - 4ac})/(2a)$$

may be obtained by a statement such as

100 X1 = (−B + SQR(B^2 − 4*A*C))/(2*A)

It is important, however, to realise that an assignment statement is not itself an equation. It is an instruction to give the variable on the left hand side the numerical value of the expression on the right hand side. Thus we may have a statement such as

50 X = X + 1

which increases by 1 the value of X.

There is no mathematical statement in common usage which is

precisely equivalent to the assignment statement

$$X = Y$$

However, in this book we shall use the symbol ':=' to denote 'becomes', so that the precisely equivalent mathematical statement is

$$x := y$$

The symbol ':=' is used in place of '=' for assignment statements in the ALGOL language.

1.3.4 *Input*

In *conversational programming* the user specifies values of variables by INPUT statements at 'run-time'. The statement has form

Line number INPUT variable 1 [, variable 2, . . .]

e.g.

20 INPUT A, B, C

When the program is run the computer prints ? on reaching this statement, and waits for the user to type values for the variables, e.g. ? 5, 10, 15 which is interpreted as A = 5, B = 10, C = 15 in the above example.

An alternative form of data input is used if there are many data, or if the data are unlikely ever to be changed, or if the user does not want to converse with the computer. In this case a statement of the form

line number READ variable 1 [, variable 2, . . .]

e.g.

20 READ A, B, C   (1.1)

is used in conjunction with a statement (or number of statements) of form

line number DATA number 1 [, number 2, . . .]

e.g. either

21 DATA 5, 10, 15   (1.2)

or

21 DATA 5
22 DATA 10   (1.3)
23 DATA 15

On executing a READ statement, values are assigned to variables from the DATA statements in the order in which the latter occur in the program. If (1.1) is followed by either (1.2) or (1.3), then A, B and C are allocated values 5, 10, and 15.

1.3.5 *Output*

The output of data (for checking purposes) and the results of calculations etc is done by a statement of form

line number PRINT list

where the list may contain variables or expressions e.g.

200 PRINT A, B, C, A*B/C

or text enclosed in quotes e.g.

10 PRINT "VALUES OF A, B, C:";

or a mixture of both e.g.

300 PRINT "X = "; X, "Y = "; Y

The items in the lists are separated by commas or semi-colons. Commas ensure a tabulation in columns about 14 spaces wide, while a semi-colon suppresses such spacing. If a semi-colon is placed at the end of a list, it suppresses the line feed. If the list is left blank then a blank line is printed, and this is a useful way of spacing out results.

Note the necessity to use PRINT statements to copy out all numbers which are input by INPUT or READ/DATA statements, so that there is a true record of them. PRINT statements should also precede INPUT statements for explanatory purposes, since ? on its own is not informative. For example the pair of statements

10 PRINT "WHAT IS X";
20 INPUT X

leads to the computer output

WHAT IS X?

in reply to which the value of X is typed in.

1.3.6 *Conditional statements*

It is often necessary to take a course of action if, and only if, some condition is fulfilled. This is done with a statement of form line number IF expression 1 $\dfrac{\text{conditional}}{\text{operator}}$ expression 2 THEN line number

where the possible 'conditional operators' are

=   equals
<> not equal to
<   less than
<= less than or equal to
>   greater than
>= greater than or equal to

For example a program could contain the following statements if it is to stop when a zero value of N is input.

$$\left.\begin{array}{l} \text{20 INPUT N} \\ \text{30 IF N <> 0 THEN 50} \\ \text{40 STOP} \\ \text{50 . . .} \end{array}\right\} \qquad (1.4)$$

Note the statement STOP which ends the run of a program. This is not to be confused with the statement END which is the (optional) last statement occurring in the program listing.

1.3.7 *Loops*

There are several ways in which a program may be made to repeat some of its procedure, and the simplest is to use the statement

line number GO TO line number

For example, if the statement

60 GO TO 20

is added to the instructions (1.4), then the program will execute statement 50 for a sequence of input values of N until a zero is input.

The most common way of doing loops is to start with a 'FOR statement'

line number FOR variable = expression 1 TO expression 2 [STEP expression 3]

where the STEP is assumed to be unity if it is omitted, and end the loop with

line number NEXT variable

The same variable is used in both FOR and NEXT statements, and its value should not be changed in the intervening statements.

A loop is used if, for example, N sets of data X, Y have to be read and a mathematical expression such as $\sin(X + Y)$ calculated in each case. e.g.

```
10 READ N
20 PRINT "X", "Y", "SIN(X + Y)"
30 FOR I = 1 TO N
40 READ X, Y
50 PRINT X, Y, SIN(X + Y)
60 NEXT I
```

Loops may also be used to calculate sums and products of a list of expressions, and this is discussed in the following chapter in connection with the symbols Σ and Π.

1.3.8 *Subscripted variables*

It is frequently desirable in mathematics to use a variable with a subscript, such as x_i, so that many cases can be covered by a simple formula. For example, we might write

$$x_i = i^2 \qquad (i = 1, 2, 3, \ldots, 10) \qquad (1.5)$$

to specify that the x_i are the squares of the integers up to 10 ($x_1 = 1, x_2 = 4, x_3 = 9, \ldots, x_{10} = 100$). In a BASIC program x_i is represented by X(I), the subscript being placed in brackets, and a specific numerical value must be assigned to I in the program, perhaps by a FOR loop. For example (1.5) may be calculated from

```
10 FOR I = 1 TO 10
20 X(I) = I^2
30 NEXT I
```

It is also permitted for a variable to have two or more subscripts attached to it. For example a matrix element a_{ij} may be represented by A(I, J).

Since a subscripted variable has more than one value associated with it (while a non-subscripted variable has just one), it is necessary to provide computer storage space for as many values as might be needed. This is done by a 'dimension statement' of the form

line number DIM variable 1 (integer 1)
[, variable 2 (integer 2), . . .]

e.g.

10 DIM X(50), Y(50), A(10, 10)

which allows up to 51 values $X(0), \ldots, X(50)$, up to 51 values $Y(0), \ldots, Y(50)$, and up to 121 values $A(0, 0), \ldots, A(10, 10)$. The DIM statement must occur before the first use of the subscripted variables.

In some computers it is possible to do 'dynamic dimensioning' with a statement like

20 DIM X(N), Y(N)

provided that N has been previously defined, and this form is useful for avoiding wasted storage space.

1.3.9 *Subroutines*

Sometimes it is necessary to use a certain sequence of statements more than once in a program, and, in order to avoid repeating these statements, it is sensible to use a subroutine for this sequence. The program then contains statements such as

line number GOSUB line number

which causes the program to transfer control to a set of instructions (the subroutine) which starts at the second line number. The subroutine must end with an instruction of form

line number RETURN

and the program then returns control from the subroutine to the statement immediately after the GOSUB call.

It is normally sensible to place subroutines at the end of a program, to keep them separate from the main body of the program.

1.3.10 *Other statements*

(a) *REM statements* are used for explanatory comments or headings in the program listing, and have the form

line number REM comment

e.g.

10 REM – THIS PROGRAM SOLVES $Y' = F(X, Y)$,
Y(0) = 1.

Such statements are ignored when the program is run. In some computers comments may be included on the same line as other statements.

(b) *String variables* enable the use of non-numeric data (e.g. words) and may be used, for example, for reading a combination of numbers and words. They will not be used in this book.

(c) *Multiple branching* can be done with statements of the form

> line number ON expression THEN line number 1
> [, line number 2, . . . ,]

or

> line number ON expression GOSUB line number 1
> [, line number 2, . . . ,]

The program transfers to the line number 1, line number 2, . . . according as the integer value of the expression is 1, 2, ...

(d) *Function definition statements* are important in mathematics since they enable us to define our own functions (in addition to built-in functions such as SIN(X)). New functions may have any of the names FNA, FNB, . . . , FNZ and are created by a statement such as

> 100 DEF FNA(X) = .5 * (EXP(X) + EXP(−X))   (1.6)

which forms the function $\cosh(x)$. DEF statements are normally placed at the end of a program. Any defined function, e.g. FNA(X) above, is simply used in the main body of the program in a statement such as

> 10 Y = FNA(1)

which sets Y equal to $\cosh(1)$ if FNA is defined by statement (1.6).

Many computers allow functions of several variables. Thus the function $f(x, y) = x^2 + y^2$ might be named in the program as FNF(X, Y) and defined by the statement

> 200 DEF FNF(X, Y) = X^2 + Y^2

1.4 Matrix routines

On many computers built-in matrix routines are available in BASIC. However, since these routines require considerable storage, they are not always available on microcomputers. Nevertheless they are a useful tool, especially in the context of matrix algebra[4].

Great care needs to be taken in the correct dimensioning of

subscripted variables referred to in matrix routines, via DIM statements. Every element A(I, J) of a matrix A with M rows and N columns has two subscripts, the row and column numbers. It is also recommended that the manual appropriate to a particular computer should be studied, since details vary between computers. For example, some computers require a vector X with 10 components to be dimensioned as X(10, 1) with 2 subscripts (i.e. 10 rows and 1 column) whenever it is to be pre-multiplied by a square matrix, say A(10, 10), while other computers permit just one subscript X(10) to be used.

The main instructions are summarised in Table 1.1.

Table 1.1 Matrix statements

Mathematics	BASIC
$A = B$	MAT A = B
$A = B + C$	MAT A = B + C
$A = B - C$	MAT A = B - C
$A = KB$ (K scalar)	MAT A = (K) * B
$A = BC$	MAT A = B * C
$A = O$ (all zeros)	MAT A = ZER
Read A	MAT READ A ⎫ Elements are listed
Input A	MAT INPUT A ⎬ individually by rows
Print A	MAT PRINT A ⎭
$A = m$ by n matrix of ones	MAT A = CON(M, N)
$A = B^T$	MAT A = TRN(B)
$A = B^{-1}$	MAT A = INV(B)
$A = I$	MAT A = IDN

Note that in matrix routines all subscripts are taken to be numbered from 1 upwards (to correspond to row or column numbers). Thus the pair of statements

    10 DIM A(10, 10)
    20 MAT INPUT A

will input 100 numbers A(1,1), . . . , A(1, 10), A(2, 1), . . . , A(10, 10).

1.5 Checking and editing programs

If a program has grammatical (syntax) errors in it, then the computer will normally give a clear indication of them. Care needs to be taken, however, to distinguish correctly between the letter 'oh' and the number 'zero' and between 'i' and 'one'. Also mystifying errors may occur if a variable is used for several purposes in the same program.

It is not of course sufficient for a program to be grammatically correct. It must give correct results. It should therefore be tested by using simple test data that give a known solution or by performing hand calculations with simple test data. It is also desirable to ensure that the program cannot go out of control for foolish choices of data, such as a negative number for the number of equations in a problem, and that it is able to cover as wide a range of potential data as possible. It is quite difficult to make programs completely 'userproof', and they become long in doing so. The programs in this book have been kept as short as possible, while providing adequate explanation, and so they are not always 'userproof'.

1.6 Different computers and variants of BASIC

The algorithms and examples in the book are programmed in a simple version of BASIC that should work on most computers, even those with small storage capacity. Only single line statements have been used, although many computers allow a number of statements on each line with a separator such as \ or :. Multiple assignments are also sometimes allowed so that, for example, the variables A, B, C, D are each set to zero by the statement

70 A = B = C = D = 0

There is one important area in which computers vary, and this is particularly relevant to microcomputers with visual display units (VDUs). This concerns the number of available columns across each line and the number of rows that are visible on the screen. Simple modifications may be necessary to fit the output of some of the programs in this book on a particular microcomputer. For this purpose TAB printing is a useful facility.

Various enhancements of BASIC have appeared over the years and these are implemented on many computer systems. Indeed the programs in this book could be re-written to incorporate some of these advanced features. For example, the availability of long variable names (e.g. ROOT instead of say X) can make it easier to write unambiguous programs, although it may be argued that one-character symbols provide a closer link with algebra. Other advanced facilities include more powerful looping with conditional statements, and independent subroutines.

Independent subroutines become particularly important in more advanced numerical mathematics where one often wishes to call upon a useful program, such as one which solves a set of linear algebraic equations, in another program[4]. This leads to the disciplines of 'structured programming', in which programs are divided into a number of smaller independent subprograms which are called upon in turn from a main 'driver' program. This greatly eases the task of debugging, since it is often possible to base a new program on a number of old well-tested subprograms. However, for the short programs in this book such good practices are not really necessary.

1.7 Summary of program contents

In writing a BASIC program, the order in which we go about listing instructions is roughly as follows:
  (i) REM statements at start (and throughout program) for explanation
 (ii) DIM statements for subscripted variables
(iii) READ/INPUT statements for data
 (iv) *Main program*, with calculations, etc
  (v) PRINT statements for results
 (vi) STOP statement to end calculation (unnecessary at the end of a program)
(vii) DEF statements for function definitions
(viii) Subroutines with RETURN statements
 (ix) END statement (optional)

1.8 References

1. J.G. Kemeny and T.E. Kurtz, *BASIC Programming*, Wiley, (1968).
2. D.M. Monro, *Interactive Computing with BASIC*, Arnold, (1974).
3. D. Alcock, *Illustrating BASIC*, Cambridge University Press, (1977).
4. J.C. Mason, *BASIC Matrix Methods*, Butterworths, (1984).

Chapter 2

Introduction to numerical mathematics

ESSENTIAL THEORY

2.1 Traditional mathematics and numerical mathematics

You will no doubt already have had a fair amount of experience of traditional mathematics, and so you will probably be wondering as you pick up this book what, if anything, you will find different about numerical mathematics. Your first impression or assumption will no doubt be that, while traditional mathematics is mostly about 'letters', numerical mathematics is mostly about 'numbers'. A first impression can often come close to the truth, and indeed there is a good measure of truth in this one, but it is not the whole story. After all there are plenty of numbers in traditional mathematics and, as you will see if you leaf through this book, there are also plenty of letters in numerical mathematics! Indeed there is much in common between traditional and numerical mathematics, and the real differences are probably more a question of emphasis and priority than of actual content. Both disciplines concern themselves with solving mathematical problems, but they do so for somewhat different reasons and with different aims in mind.

In both traditional and numerical mathematics, a mathematical problem is studied from a number of points of view, and various questions are asked about the solution(s) such as the following:

Does the problem have solutions?
Is there just one solution?
What is the nature of the solution?

However, in considering the last question the traditional mathematician is likely to be more concerned in establishing that the solution *can* be found than in actually finding it. Moreover, any constructions that he gives for the solution are likely to be designed primarily to establish the structure and properties of the solution rather than to determine all of its values rapidly. In contrast, numerical mathematics has developed with the specific aim of actually solving problems and printing out the answers.

Many of the methods involved in numerical mathematics have

only become possible to implement as a result of the development of electronic computers and silicon chips, and conversely the development of better computers has led to a demand for more and better numerical mathematics. However, it would be wrong to see numerical mathematics as a replacement for traditional mathematics. Engineers and scientists need the complementary aspects of both traditional and numerical mathematics. Moreover numerical mathematics itself has its roots in traditional mathematics, and many of the 'new' methods it uses are based on ideas developed within traditional mathematics.

Making a more specific comparison between numerical and traditional mathematics, the two main differences of emphasis concern (i) exactness of solutions and (ii) effectiveness of methods. The traditional mathematician studies the *exact solution* of a problem, the determination of which often involves an *infinite process*. For example, the number of times that the diameter of a circle divides its circumference is exactly equal to π, a number with an infinite decimal representation (3.14159265...). However, no computer can perform an infinite number of calculations, and so this exact solution (π) cannot ever be calculated. Similarly, in constructing a *method* of solution, the traditional mathematician is often as concerned with *structure and elegance* as he is with efficiency and reliability, although constraints of computer time and cost may in practice dictate that efficiency should be given higher priority.

The aims of the numerical mathematician, in contrast to those of the traditional mathematician are (i) to solve a problem *approximately* in a *finite* number of steps, and (ii) to obtain the solution by a method which is *efficient and reliable*.

Let us consider some examples which illustrate these ideas.

Example 2.1: Integration

Suppose that it is required to calculate the integral $\int_0^t \exp(-x^2)\, \mathrm{d}x$ for some specified positive value of t. Indeed tables of values of this integral for various values of t are commonly needed for statistical calculations where a 'normal distribution of probabilities' is assumed. However, we soon discover that we cannot obtain a formula for the integral by using standard analytical techniques of integration (such as integration by parts, etc). We must either use some kind of infinite series representation for the integral and integrate this term by term, or look for a numerical method. Moreover this integral is not uncommonly difficult. Indeed there are in general surprisingly few functions which can be integrated analytically, and numerical methods are frequently required. The idea of most numerical methods is to approximately calculate the area under the graph of the integrand $y = \exp(-x^2)$ between $x = 0$ and t, as indicated by the shaded area in Figure 2.1. Such methods are discussed fully in a later chapter.

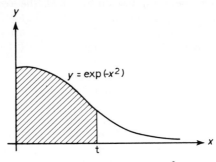

Figure 2.1 Integral of $\exp(-x^2)$

Example 2.2: Nonlinear equations

The problem of determining the solution x (in radians) of the equation

$$\tan x = 2x \qquad (0 < x < \pi/2) \qquad (2.1)$$

which occurs in connection with the conduction of heat in a solid (subject to radiation applied at its boundaries)[1], cannot be solved exactly in a finite number of steps. Indeed the true solution

$$x = s = 1.1656\ldots$$

is an 'irrational' number (rather like π) with a never-ending decimal representation. By sketching the graphs of $y = \tan x$ and $y = 2x$ and considering their intersections, or alternatively by using some elementary calculus, a traditional mathematician immediately deduces that equation (2.1) has a unique solution s between $\pi/4$ and $\pi/2$ (see Figure 2.2). (Note that the solution $x = 0$ has been disallowed by restricting x to the range $0 < x < \pi/2$ in (2.1).) He may then subsequently simply refer to this solution by the letter s and produce formulae for the temperature in the solid at a given position and time in terms of s. However, the numerical mathematician is left with the task of calculating an actual value of s, and he must do so in a finite number of steps to a required accuracy as efficiently as possible. This type of problem is also discussed in a later chapter.

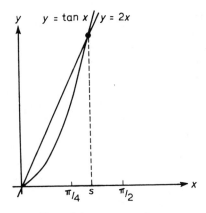

Figure 2.2 $y = \tan x = 2x$

Example 2.3: Simultaneous equations

We are all familiar from school mathematics with the problem of solving a pair of simultaneous equations for x_1 and x_2.

$$a_{11}x_1 + a_{12}x_2 = b_1$$
$$a_{21}x_1 + a_{22}x_2 = b_2 \tag{2.2}$$

where $a_{11}, a_{12}, a_{21}, a_{22}, b_1, b_2$ are given numbers. The solution may be obtained in a number of ways, and it is easy to verify the validity of the following elegant formula based on determinants:

$$\frac{x_1}{\begin{vmatrix} b_1 & a_{12} \\ b_2 & a_{22} \end{vmatrix}} = \frac{x_2}{\begin{vmatrix} a_{11} & b_1 \\ a_{21} & b_2 \end{vmatrix}} = \frac{1}{\begin{vmatrix} a_{11} & a_{12} \\ a_{21} & a_{22} \end{vmatrix}} \tag{2.3}$$

This formula generalises very nicely to provide us with a formula called 'Cramer's rule' for the solution of a set of any number n of simultaneous equations in n unknowns $x_1, x_2, \ldots, x_n$. The problem generalises to:

$$a_{11}x_1 + a_{12}x_2 + \cdots + a_{1n}x_n = b_1$$
$$a_{21}x_1 + a_{22}x_2 + \cdots + a_{2n}x_n = b_2$$
$$\vdots \qquad \vdots \qquad \qquad \vdots \tag{2.4}$$
$$a_{n1}x_1 + a_{n2}x_2 + \cdots + a_{nn}x_n = b_n$$

where $a_{11}, \ldots, a_{nn}, b_1, \ldots, b_n$ are given coefficients, and the formula becomes

$$
\frac{x_1}{\begin{vmatrix} b_1 a_{12} a_{13} & \cdots & a_{1n} \\ b_2 a_{22} a_{23} & \cdots & a_{2n} \\ \vdots & & \vdots \\ b_n a_{n2} a_{n3} & \cdots & a_{nn} \end{vmatrix}} = \frac{x_2}{\begin{vmatrix} a_{11} b_1 a_{13} & \cdots & a_{1n} \\ a_{21} b_2 a_{23} & \cdots & a_{2n} \\ \vdots & & \vdots \\ a_{n1} b_n a_{n3} & \cdots & a_{nn} \end{vmatrix}} =
$$

$$
\cdots = \frac{x_n}{\begin{vmatrix} a_{11} & \cdots & a_{1,n-1} b_1 \\ a_{21} & \cdots & a_{2,n-1} b_2 \\ \vdots & & \vdots \\ a_{n1} & \cdots & a_{n,n-1} b_n \end{vmatrix}} = \frac{1}{\begin{vmatrix} a_{11} a_{12} & \cdots & a_{1n} \\ a_{21} a_{22} & \cdots & a_{2n} \\ \vdots & & \vdots \\ a_{n1} a_{n2} & \cdots & a_{nn} \end{vmatrix}} \tag{2.5}
$$

Although the formula (2.5) appears to have demolished the equations (2.4), a different picture emerges on counting up the number of multiplications involved. By expanding each determinant in terms of determinants of lower order, it is not difficult to deduce (by induction) that (2.5) involves $(n + 1)!$ multiplications or divisions, which amounts to over thirty million in the case $n = 10$. However, equations (2.4) may equally well be solved numerically by the 'Gauss elimination' method[2], similar in spirit to the elementary school method of solving (2.2), in which variables are repeatedly eliminated from the equations until they can be solved by substitution. This method involves only about $n^3/3$ multiplications or divisions, which is about three hundred in the case $n = 10$. Thus, in efficiency, the inelegant Gauss elimination method is enormously superior (100 000 times as fast for $n = 10$) to the elegant Cramer's rule.

This is not meant as a slander on Cramer's rule! Although it should not be used for actually calculating the solution $x_1, x_2, \ldots, x_n$ (except in simple cases such as $n = 2$ or $n = 3$), it is still a valuable mathematical tool for the study of general algebraic properties of systems of simultaneous equations and of the matrices and determinants associated with them.

2.2 Numerical methods and numerical analysis

If you look in the shelves of a library, you will find a variety of textbooks on numerical mathematics. Books intended for scientists, engineers, and other 'practical' people tend to be given a title like 'numerical methods', while books intended for mathematicians, graduate students, and other 'highbrow' people tend to be given a title like 'numerical analysis'. Numerical methods and numerical analysis are indeed the two main aspects of numerical mathematics, and their tasks are essentially as follows:

Numerical methods
Find a *method* for obtaining a numerical solution of a problem.

Numerical analysis
Analyse the properties of the method and the *errors* in the computed solution.

Obviously both these topics are relevant in all textbooks, and a greater emphasis is given to one or other to suit the reader. However, there is a misconception amongst some engineers and scientists that they need only concern themselves with numerical methods, and that numerical analysis is for mathematicians to worry about. They assume that all well-known or popular methods will probably work, especially if they are included in computer program library. Any vices in a method will presumably become obvious once the method has been tried out. Neither of these assumptions is correct. When faced with a battery of methods which purport to solve a certain problem, it is better to make a choice based on analysis (someone else's if necessary) than to base one's choice on a random guess. A prominent professor of engineering mathematics was recently quoted as saying that "it is inexcusable that an engineer should not take numerical analysis into account".

How then do we analyse numerical methods? Ideally we estimate or calculate the errors in the numerical solutions obtained by a variety of methods. We then choose *the method which achieves a required accuracy by the shortest calculation*. Clearly a key factor in this is to be able to understand and recognise all the types of errors which may occur during a calculation. However, before categorising these errors, we must first introduce essential facts about such fundamental ideas as decimal and binary numbers, fixed-point and floating-point arithmetic, and absolute and relative errors.

2.3 Decimal and binary numbers

We are all of course familiar with decimal representations of rational (i.e. fractional) numbers such as

$$47/4 = 11.75 \quad = (1 \times 10^1) + (1 \times 10^0) + (7 \times 10^{-1}) + (5 \times 10^{-2})$$
$$8/3 = 2.666\ldots = (2 \times 10^0) + (6 \times 10^{-1}) + (6 \times 10^{-2}) + (6 \times 10^{-3}) + \cdots$$

Here *base ten* is used, with the set of ten numerical symbols $0, 1, 2, \ldots, 9$. We are also familiar with methods for adding, multiplying, subtracting, and dividing such numbers.

However, ten is not the only possible base to use, and indeed most electronic computers adopt *base two*, with *binary* representations of numbers such as

$$47/4 = 1011.11 \quad = (1 \times 2^3) + (0 \times 2^2) + (1 \times 2^1) + (1 \times 2^0)$$
$$+ (1 \times 2^{-1}) + (1 \times 2^{-2}),$$
$$8/3 = 10.1010\ldots = (1 \times 2^1) + (0 + 2^0) + (1 \times 2^{-1}) + (0 \times 2^{-2})$$
$$+ \cdots$$

Only two numerical symbols 0 and 1 are used in binary, and as a result additions and multiplications are extremely straightforward to perform:

$$1 + 1 = 10, \quad 111 \times 101 = 11100 + 111 = 100011, \text{ etc.}$$

Indeed if such numbers were used in everyday life, children might well find arithmetic easier to do! Nevertheless, decimal numbers are much more convenient for human communications where brevity is important. For example telephone numbers, which already extend to 9 or more decimal digits (including area codes), would become absurd if converted into 30 binary digits – ring me on

$$1111010011011101111101011000111 \ !$$

However, electronic computers with their automatic memories are not affected by such considerations, and the use of binary processes in their arithmetic units has been a key factor in the computer revolution.

Since computers are servants of humans (and definitely not vice versa!) computer 'software' is usually designed to give us the outward impression that the computer is operating in decimals. This enables us to have the best of both worlds: we communicate with the computer as if it were a decimal machine, while the computer itself operates in binary. (Incidentally, much the same principle applies to programming languages such as BASIC. We communicate with the computer in BASIC, because it suits us, while the computer itself operates in a language of its own.) It is therefore reasonable for decimals only to be used throughout this textbook, even in dealing with topics (such as rounding error) in which the laws are based on properties of binary numbers. Although the details may not always in consequence be quantitatively precise, the ideas and principles are still qualitatively correct.

2.4 Fixed-point and floating-point arithmetic

Since storage space in a calculation is likely to be limited, it is usual to work either to a *fixed number of decimal places* or to a *fixed number of significant figures*. This makes it necessary at various stages to 'round' numbers to these accuracies. All superfluous digits are erased, and the last required digit is rounded according to the following rules.

Rules for rounding:
(i)   Leave the last required digit unchanged if the following digits are below 5000...
(ii) Add one to the last required digit if the following digits exceed 5000...
(iii) Leave the last required digit unchanged or add one to it, according as it is even or odd, if the following digits are exactly 5000...

For example,

$$
\begin{aligned}
0.173 &= 0.17 &&\text{to 2 decimal places,}\\
1.73284 &= 1.733 &&\text{to 3 decimal places,}\\
31.205 &= 31.20 &&\text{to 4 significant figures,}\\
17.2775 &= 17.278 &&\text{to 5 significant figures.}
\end{aligned}
$$

Readers are almost certainly familiar with the phrases 'correct to 3 decimal places' and 'correct to 4 significant figures'. However, there is some difference of opinion as to their meaning. For example, some people would say that, as an approximation to π (3.14159265...), the number 3.1416 is not correct to 4 decimal places since the figure 6 is incorrect. This we would regard as an absurd line of argument, since 3.1415 is even less correct! The following precise definitions will therefore be used:

(i)   A number is *correct to p decimal places* if it has an error of at most 5 in the $(p + 1)$th decimal place.
(ii) A number is *correct to q significant figures* if it has an error of at most 5 in the $(q + 1)$th significant figure.

For example, if the solution to a problem is 0.5446, then 0.545 is correct to 3 significant figures and 0.54 is correct to 2 decimal places. Note that the maximum errors permitted in these definitions (5 in the next digit) are precisely the maximum errors which may occur in rounding to the given number of decimal places or significant figures.

On early computers it was quite common to use *fixed-point* *arithmetic* (so called because the decimal point is kept in a fixed position) in which a *fixed number of decimal places* is retained in every number both before and after each addition, multiplication, etc. For example, if two decimal places are retained, then the multiplication

$$6543.21 \times 0.014$$

proceeds as follows:

$$6543.21 \times 0.014 = 6543.21 \times 0.01 = 65.4321 = 65.43.$$

However, the *exact* calculation would be as follows:

$$6543.21 \times 0.014 = 91.60494 \ (= 91.60 \text{ to 2 dec. pl.}),$$

and so fixed-point arithmetic can give very inaccurate results.

To avoid disastrous results such as this, numbers in fixed-point arithmetic need to be kept carefully scaled. Some forethought and skill is involved in this, and so it is probably fortunate that fixed-point arithmetic is not encouraged on modern computers, although the facility is still available on many desk calculators. Instead calculations nowadays are normally executed in floating-point arithmetic (so called because the decimal point is allowed to 'float' from one position to another) in which a *fixed number of significant figures* is retained both before and after each arithmetic operation. The decimal point in each number is shifted to the immediate left of the first non-zero digit, and an appropriate multiplying power of 10 is attached after the number. This power of 10 is just the number of decimal places that the decimal place has been shifted to the left, and it is called the 'exponent' of the number. For example, in 6 decimal floating-point arithmetic

$$6543.21 \ = 0.654321 \times 10^4 \ = 0.654321 \text{ E } 4,$$
$$0.014 = 0.140000 \times 10^{-1} = 0.140000 \text{ E}-1,$$
$$0.5 \ \ = 0.500000 \times 10^0 \ = 0.500000 \text{ E } 0.$$

The shorthand notation E4, which stands for 'times ten to the power of 4' (with the letter E for exponent) is commonly used. If the first two numbers are multiplied in 6 decimal floating-point, the calculation is as follows:

$$\begin{aligned}
0.654321 \ E4 \times 0.140000 \ E-1 &= (0.654321 \times 10^4) \times \\
&\times (0.140000 \times 10^{-1}) = (0.654321 \times 0.140000)10^{4-1} \\
&= (0.09160494) \times 10^3 = 0.916049 \times 10^2 = 0.916049 \ E2
\end{aligned}$$

Note that *floating-point* arithmetic is effectively a way of incorporating *automatic scaling* into fixed-point arithmetic, all numbers being multipled by appropriate powers of 10 to keep them always between 0 and 1.

Some textbooks and computers standardise floating-point numbers in a slightly different way from that above by writing one digit before the decimal point, such as $1.23456\,E-3$ instead of $0.123456\,E-2$. This has the advantage that the number can be interpreted immediately as 'about 1 in the 3rd decimal place', and it has the disadvantage of not being as 'tidy' as the notation adopted by us!

Notice that in storing a floating-point number, some space has to be occupied by the exponent. This means that, for a fixed 'word-length' computer, numbers cannot be expressed to as many figures in floating-point arithmetic as in fixed-point arithmetic, and so some accuracy is lost. For example, on a calculator with a word-length (i.e. a display) of 12 digits we can store either the fixed-point number 654321.234567 (with 12 significant figures) or the equivalent floating-point number $.65432123\,E+06$ (with 8 significant figures). Four figures are allocated for E, a sign, and a two digit exponent.

2.5 Absolute and relative errors

If a number x is calculated only approximately as another number x^*, then the error in x may be expressed in three ways: as an absolute error, a relative error, or a percentage error.

(i)   *The absolute error* in x, or the *absolute accuracy* of x, is the magnitude of the discrepancy:

$$|x - x^*|$$

(ii)   The *relative error* in x, or *relative accuracy* of x, is the ratio of the absolute error to x:

$$|(x - x^*)/x| \quad \text{or} \quad |1 - x^*/x|$$

(Note that the relative error is not defined for $x = 0$.)

(iii)   The *percentage error*, or *percentage accuracy*, is the relative error scaled so as to lie between 0 and 100:

$$100\,|(x - x^*)/x| \text{ per cent}$$

These definitions may be usefully illustrated in connection with the rounding of numbers. For example, if a fixed-point number is rounded as follows:

$$0.003125 = 0.00312 \quad \text{(to 5 decimal places)},$$

the absolute, relative, and percentage errors are respectively

$$0.000005, \quad 0.0016, \quad \text{and} \quad 0.16 \text{ per cent.}$$

Similarly, if a floating-point number is rounded as follows:

$$0.100005 \text{ E7} = 0.10000 \text{ E7} \quad \text{(to 5 significant figures),}$$

the absolute, relative, and percentage errors are respectively (in floating-point)

$$0.50000 \text{ E2}, \quad 0.49997 \text{ E}-4, \quad \text{and} \quad 0.49997 \text{ E}-2 \text{ per cent.}$$

Note that these two examples have been chosen to exhibit the worst possible absolute error and relative error, respectively.

If we are interested in absolute accuracy, then this is most easily determined if results are expressed to a certain number of decimal places. Specifically, if we round a number to p decimal places then the absolute error is at most 5 in the $(p + 1)$th decimal place (e.g. 5 in the 6th decimal place for 5 decimals in the first example above). Thus the absolute error is comparable with the number of decimal places used.

However, if we are interested in relative accuracy, then this is most easily determined if results are expressed to a certain number of significant figures. Specifically, if we round a number to q significant figures then the relative error is at most 5 in the qth significant figure (e.g. 5 in the 5th figure, that is, .00005, for 5 significant figures in the second example above). Thus the relative error is comparable with the number of significant figures used.

2.6 Errors in numerical calculations

Having now discussed the fundamentals of accuracy and error, let us consider the complete variety of ways in which errors may enter into a numerical solution. Such errors occur regardless of the tool which is used for the calculation, be it a computer, a desk calculator, a set of log tables, a slide rule, or our head. The errors may be classified in four categories:

 (i) human errors
(ii) errors in the data
(iii) truncation errors
(iv) rounding errors.

Categories (i) and (ii) speak for themselves. In categories (iii) and (iv), truncation error is the error caused by terminating a potentially infinite calculation after only a finite number of steps, and rounding error is the error due to performing calculations to a fixed number of significant figures. The four categories are discussed in more detail with illustrative examples in the following subsections.

In discussing the last three categories of errors three important ideas of numerical analysis are introduced: conditioning, convergence and stability. Fortunately in most of the problems considered in this textbook, no more than one or two of these types of errors tend to occur at the same time, and so it is normally possible to isolate each type of error without difficulty.

2.6.1 *Human errors*

The first of the four types of errors which may occur is so obvious that there is a tendency to either ignore it or feel too embarrassed to mention it! A human error or *blunder*, namely any slip made during the course of the calculation, is probably the most common form of error. It could be an inadvertent error in copying down or typing out the data, an error in a desk calculation, an error in a computer program, or even an error in a mathematical formula. If a numerical method fails unexpectedly, then a human error is the most likely cause. Never blame a method until you have made quite certain that you have eliminated all human errors, or you may make yourself unpopular!

Human errors can be the most difficult of the four types of errors to trace. On the whole they are fairly easy to recognise because they tend to produce much larger errors in the solution of the problem than do other types of errors, though they can also on occasion produce very small errors. Human errors in computer programs are quite a common occurrence, and the finding of such errors (sometimes called 'debugging') can be a tiresome exercise until some experience and practice has been gained. Human errors commonly occur also in implementing methods and formulae from textbooks. It is easy to neglect some part of a method, to misinterpret the method, or to mix up the symbols for the various unknowns. Moreover textbooks are not infallible, and it is worthwhile either to crosscheck a formula between two textbooks or to verify the analysis that leads to the formula. These remarks must also apply to the textbook which you are reading at this very moment!

Just as textbooks which it is tempting to regard as 'true' are not infallible, so computer library programs which are sometimes treated with reverence may have errors in them. Indeed it has been known for small errors, which only occur with occasional sets of data, to lie unnoticed in computer library programs for some years.

One of the best ways to test a computer program is to run it with a set of test data, corresponding to a simple special case, and then to compare the resulting numerical results with those obtained by doing the same calculation on a desk calculator. This is a discipline which is advocated throughout this book.

2.6.2 *Errors in the data (and conditioning)*

Often the data of a problem are inexact, either because they are physical measurements or because they are simply given to a limited accuracy. Errors are then introduced into the data, producing consequent errors in the solution. The latter may or may not be large, depending on what is termed the 'conditioning of the problem'. If a small error in the data leads to a large error in the solution then the problem is said to be *ill-conditioned*, and if it only leads to a small error in the solution then the problem is said to be *well-conditioned*.

Consider for example the following problems:

Problem A:
Determine to an absolute accuracy of 0.0001 a solution x of the quadratic equation

$$x^2 - 1.0640x + 0.2830 = 0. \qquad (2.6)$$

By using the standard formula for solutions of a quadratic, we deduce that

$$x = (-b \pm \sqrt{b^2 - 4ac})/(2a)$$

where $a = 1$, $b = -1.0640$, $c = 0.2830$, i.e. $x = 0.5271$ and 0.5369 (to 4 decimal places). Now if the coefficient 1.0640 is changed to 1.0641, a *small change of 0.0001* in the data, then the solutions become

$$x = 0.5233 \quad \text{and} \quad 0.5408$$

corresponding to a *large change of 0.004* in the solutions. Problem A is therefore ill-conditioned.

When a problem is ill-conditioned, it is clear that a much lower accuracy must be expected in the solution than is present in the data. For example it is unrealistic to expect four correct figures in a solution just because four correct figures are given in the problem. Indeed if the coefficients in (2.6) are correct to only 4 decimal places then Problem A *cannot be solved* as posed.

Strangely enough, ill-conditioning can be made to disappear magically, if the problem is simply posed in a slightly different way!

Problem B:
Determine a value of x such that the quadratic

$$y(x) = x^2 - 1.0640x + 0.2830 \qquad (2.7)$$

is equal to zero to an absolute accuracy of 0.0001.

We know $y(x)$ is zero for $x = 0.5271$ or 0.5369 (the 'exact' solutions of (2.6)). Now if 1.0640 is changed to 1.0641, then the equation to be solved is

$$y^*(x) = x^2 - 1.0641x + 0.2830 = y(x) - 0.0001x = 0$$

and so $y^*(x)$ and $y(x)$ differ by only about .00005 for $x = .5271$ or .5369. Both of these x values are therefore acceptable solutions of the equation $y^*(x) = 0$. Indeed it is not difficult to verify that $y(x)$ is zero to an absolute accuracy of 0.0001 (i.e. $y(x)$ lies between -0.0001 and $+0.0001$) for any values of x between 0.522 and 0.542, and so any choice of x in this range is acceptable. A set of values of $y(x)$ against x are printed in Table 2.1 to illustrate this point. Problem B is in fact well-conditioned.

Table 2.1 Values of $y = x^2 - 1.0640x + 0.2830$

x	y	x	y
0.0	0.283000	0.532	−0.000024
0.1	0.186600	0.534	−0.000020
0.2	0.110200	0.536	−0.000008
0.3	0.053800	0.538	0.000012
0.4	0.017400	0.540	0.000040
0.5	0.001000	0.542	0.000076
0.520	0.000120	0.544	0.000120
0.522	0.000076	0.6	0.004600
0.524	0.000040	0.7	0.028200
0.526	0.000012	0.8	0.071800
0.528	−0.000008	0.9	0.135400
0.530	−0.000020	1.0	0.219000

So we see from this example that by posing a problem in a slightly different way we may change it from an ill-conditioned problem (which is difficult to solve accurately unless data are very accurate) to a well-conditioned problem. If in a 'real world situation' we were posed Problem A above, we would point out to the poser that it was difficult to solve and ask him if he had any real objection to us solving Problem B instead. He might well say that Problem B was the one he really wanted to have solved in the first place. Indeed, in a physical problem it is often more important to satisfy an equation of state or motion accurately than it is to determine a set of values of the solution accurately.

2.6.3 *Truncation errors (and convergence)*

A numerical method involves by necessity only a finite number, n say, of steps, while the true solution may involve an infinite process of calculation. If it does, then an error is bound to be produced in the numerical method itself by 'truncating' the infinite process into a finite one, and this error is therefore called *truncation error*. If the true solution is y, and the numerical solution obtained by a calculation with only n steps is y_n, then the truncation error is

$$y - y_n$$

In practice n is increased until y is obtained to an acceptable accuracy. For this to be possible the truncation error must approach zero as n becomes larger. In other words y_n must *converge* to y as n 'tends to infinity', and so the numerical idea of truncation error is linked directly to the mathematical idea of convergence.

Suppose for example that y is equal to e, the base of natural logarithms, and is calculated by using the infinite series expansion

$$y = \mathrm{e} = 1 + \frac{1}{1!} + \frac{1}{2!} + \frac{1}{3!} + \frac{1}{4!} + \cdots + \frac{1}{n!} + \cdots \qquad (2.8)$$

Let y_n denote the series truncated after n additions, so that

$$y_n = 1 + \frac{1}{1!} + \frac{1}{2!} + \cdots + \frac{1}{n!} \qquad (2.9)$$

is a numerical approximation to y for a suitable choice of n. Then the truncation error is $y - y_n$, and in this case by subtracting (2.9) from (2.8) we obtain the formula

$$y - y_n = \frac{1}{(n + 1)!} + \frac{1}{(n + 2)!} + \cdots \qquad (2.10)$$

In Table 2.2 are given the values $y_0, y_1, \ldots, y_9$ of y_n for $n = 0$, $1, \ldots, 9$, all correct to five significant figures. It is clear that these values are approaching the fixed value $2.7183\ldots$, namely e, as n increases, and in fact y_n is converging to y as n tends to infinity.

The truncation error cannot be calculated conveniently from (2.10), which is yet another infinite series. However, from Table

Table 2.2 Values of y_n

n	y_n	n	y_n
0	1.0000	5	2.7167
1	2.0000	6	2.7181
2	2.5000	7	2.7183
3	2.6667	8	2.7183
4	2.7084	9	2.7183

2.2 we can deduce that $e \simeq 2.7183$ and hence that for $n = 5$, for example, the truncation error is

$$y - y_5 \simeq 2.7183 - 2.7167 = 0.0016$$

Note that this value of $y - y_5$ is only correct to about two significant figures, since three figures have been lost in the subtraction. Moreover, in the case $n = 9$, the truncation error is

$$y - y_9 \simeq 2.7183 - 2.7183 = 0.0000$$

and this value does not have a single correct significant figure. (This is an example of 'significance error' which is discussed in the following section.) However, since y_7, y_8 and y_9 all agree to 4 decimals, it is reasonable to estimate that

$$-0.0001 < y - y_9 < 0.0001$$

although this is not a rigorous mathematical deduction!

So, even if it is not always possible to calculate the truncation error, we can often make reasonable estimates of it based on the actual numerical results.

2.6.4 *Rounding errors (and stability)*

If a desk calculator or a computer is used for numerical calculations, then, as was pointed out above, floating point arithmetic (a fixed number of significant figures) is normally used. This means that the result of every arithmetic operation has to be rounded to the machine accuracy, and the error so produced is termed *rounding error*. On a desk calculator numbers are rounded to the length of the visual display, which is typically about 10 significant figures. On a computer, the result of every BASIC arithmetic operation is generally rounded to between 6 and 8 significant figures (depending on the word length of the computer). The net effect of all of the rounding performed during the course of the calculation is termed the *accumulated rounding error*, and it may have a noticeable effect on the final result.

The way in which rounding is performed is very much dependent on the design of the 'arithmetic unit' in the 'hardware' of the particular brand of computer or calculator used, and this makes it difficult to predict accurately the precise way in which this error will accumulate. However, it is possible to determine bounds on the rounding error, based either on the worst possible accumulations or on the statistically most likely accumulations. Although the 'worst possible' bounds are likely to be very pessimistic, they are easier to calculate than statistical estimates and are often quite useful from a qualitative point of view. In practice it is sometimes possible to assess rounding error by observing obvious inconsistencies in the actual calculated results, and this is a very convenient method when applicable.

Let us see first how rounding errors occur in fundamental arithmetic operations. Suppose that our calculating machine retains exactly 6 significant decimal figures. (Most computers operate in binary numbers, rather than decimal numbers, but the effect is essentially the same.) Then a typical *multiplication* is a follows.

$$6.54321 \times 1.00001 = 6.5432754321$$
$$= 6.54328 \text{ (rounding the 6th digit)}$$

In the above example the rounding error is equal to 0.0000045679. Clearly the worst rounding error that can ever be made in one multiplication is 5 in the first neglected decimal figure.

In a typical *addition*, with the same calculating machine,

$$6.54321 + 0.00543216 = 6.54864216$$
$$= 6.54864 \text{ (rounding the 6th digit)}$$

Again there is in general a rounding error of at worst 5 in the first neglected decimal place.

It is not difficult to show that similar rounding errors occur in *division* and *subtraction*, and that again they each contribute at worst 5 in the first neglected decimal place.

However, this is not the complete story, since we must also consider how rounding errors *accumulate* from one calculation to the next. This topic is generally beyond the scope of this discussion. However, there are two special situations which will be illustrated since they are potentially extremely serious: instability, and significance error.

A method is said to be *unstable* if the accumulated rounding error grows relative to the values of the solution as we increase the number m of values calculated. If rounding error does not grow, the method is stable.

Consider, for example, the calculation of the numbers x_2 x_3, x_4, . . . defined by the recurrence

$$x_i = 10.1x_{i-1} - x_{i-2} \qquad i = 2, 3, 4, \ldots \qquad (2.11)$$

where $x_0 = 1.001$, $x_1 = 0.1$. The values of the solution may in principle be calculated exactly from Equation (2.11) (without truncation error), and so rounding error is the only potential source of error. In Table 2.3 are given the true values of x_0, x_1, x_2, . . ., and also the values $x_0^*, x_1^*, x_2^*, \ldots$ which are computed from Equation (2.11) in 3 decimal floating-point arithmetic. Clearly the use of the recurrence (2.11) is *unstable*. Indeed the values of $x_3^*, x_4^*, x_5^*, \ldots$ do not even remotely resemble those of $x_3, x_4, x_5, \ldots$!

Table 2.3 Solutions x_i of the recurrence (2.11)

i	x_i (exact)	x_i^* (3 dec. arithmetic)	Rounding error
0	1.001	1.00	0.1%
1	0.1	0.1	0%
2	0.009	0.01	11%
3	−0.0091	0.001	111%
4	−0.10091	0.0001	100%
5	−1.010091	0.00001	100%

The dangerous phenomenon of *significance error* occurs even more suddenly. Suppose a subtraction such as the following is performed:

$$6.54321 - 6.54320 = 0.00001 \qquad (2.12)$$

where 6.54321 and 6.54320 already contain rounding errors. Although no new rounding error as such is created here, the actual calculation takes a pair of numbers rounded to 6 figures and subtracts them to give a number with just one significant figure. The 'true' calculation might, for example, be

$$6.5432149 - 6.5431950 = 0.0000199,$$

and in that case the resulting error in Equation (2.12) would be about 100 per cent! Such a disastrous type of accumulation of rounding error is called *significance error*. It is caused by the subtraction of two nearly equal numbers with a consequent 'loss of significance' (i.e. loss of significant figures).

In general if we subtract two numbers which have rounding errors of at worst 5 in the pth significant figure and which have q leading figures in common, then the result can be in error by at worst 1 in the $(p-q-1)$th significant figure. (In the example (2.12) above, $p = 7$, $q = 5$, and so the error is at worst 1 in the first figure.)

Examples of significance errors in quadratic equations

Example (i)   Significance error is further illustrated in the determination of the solution x of the quadratic equation (2.6), that is

$$x^2 - 1.0640 + 0.2830 = 0.$$

We have already shown this to be an ill-conditioned problem (see Problem A above). Let us now suppose that the data of the problem is exact, but that the solutions are calculated using just 4 significant decimal figures throughout. Using the standard formula for the roots of a quadratic, the calculation proceeds as follows:

$$\begin{aligned}
x &= (1.064 \pm \sqrt{(1.064)^2 - 4(0.2830)})/2 \\
&= (1.064 \pm \sqrt{(1.132096 - 1.132)})/2 \\
&= (1.064 \pm \sqrt{(1.132 - 1.132)})/2 \\
&= 0.532 \pm 0
\end{aligned}$$

The true solutions are, however, $x = 0.5271, 0.5369$ and so an error of 0.0049, or about one per cent, occurs in each solution. The source of the error is of course significance error, due to cancellation within the square root. A true (but small) value of 0.000096 is replaced by 0, which means that on taking square roots a true (but no longer small) value of 0.0098 is replaced by 0. The consequent error is finally divided by 2 to give an error of 0.0049.

In general, significance error inside the square root in the solution of a quadratic can lose up to half the number of decimal figures of the data (2 out of 4 figures in this example). However, even worse significance errors can occur at a later stage of the calculation, as we see in the following example.

Example (ii)   Consider the quadratic equation

$$x^2 - 300x + 1 = 0 \qquad (2.13)$$

and suppose that the two solutions are required to four significant figures using just four significant figures in the arithmetic. By the standard formula, the calculation proceeds as follows.

$$x = (300 \pm \sqrt{(90\ 000 - 4)})/2$$
$$= (300 \pm \sqrt{(90\ 000)})/2$$
$$= (300 \pm 300)/2$$
$$= 300, 0$$

However, the true solutions are $x = 300.0, 0.003333$, and so the numerical method has not produced a single significant figure in the smaller solution. This is a result of significance error in subtracting from 300 the very nearly equal number $\sqrt{89996}$.

Curiously enough these difficulties in the problem disappear if we calculate the smaller root by observing that the product of the two roots x_1, x_2 must equal the constant term 1 in Equation (2.13). Thus the smaller root is

$$x_2 = 1/x_1 = 1/300 = 0.003333$$

to 4 significant figures.

In general the only way to eliminate significance error from a calculation is to find another method of performing the calculation, just as we have done in Example (ii). However, there is very little that can be done to obtain full accuracy in Example (i), owing to the closeness of the two roots, except perhaps to use a larger number of significant figures in the calculations within the square root.

2.7 Summary of key ideas and concepts

To complete this discussion, the various steps that constitute an *ideal* numerical method have been summarised in one diagram (Figure 2.3) together with the various questions which should be answered if possible. It is hoped that this will provide a useful reference, and that after finishing this book you will have some idea of how to answer some of these questions for at least some methods!

A number of new concepts have also been introduced in this Chapter, and these are listed below for convenience:

Definitions of key concepts

Truncation error   Error caused by terminating a numerical method after a finite number of (n) steps.

Rounding error   Error caused by inexact arithmetic, i.e. only allowing a fixed number of decimal places in a calculation.

Well-posed problem (opposite: ill-posed problem)   A problem which has a unique and meaningful solution.

Well-conditioned/ill-conditioned problem: A problem is well/ill conditioned if a small change in the data leads to a small/large change in the solution.

Convergent methods (opposite: divergent)   A numerical method is convergent if the solution computed after n steps of the method tends to the true solution of the problem as $n \to \infty$ (i.e. truncation error $\to 0$).

Stable/unstable method   A numerical method is stable/unstable if the accumulated rounding error does not grow/does grow relative to the solution as we increase the number of values calculated.

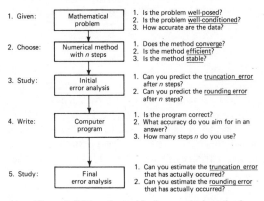

Figure 2.3 Steps in an ideal numerical method

2.8 Further reading

The discussion in this chapter is intended to provide a brief but useful introduction. A deeper treatment of error analysis and floating point arithmetic is given in the practical text of L. Fox and D.F. Mayers[3]. As far as rounding errors in particular are concerned, the rigorous introductory text of J.H. Wilkinson[4] is to be recommended.

2.9 References

1. H.S. Carslaw and J.C. Jaeger, *Conduction of Heat in Solids* 2 ed, Clarendon Press, (1959).
2. J.C. Mason, *BASIC Matrix Methods*, Butterworths, (1984).
3. L. Fox and D.F. Mayers, *Computing Methods for Scientists and Engineers*, Oxford University Press, (1968).
4. J.H. Wilkinson, *Rounding Errors in Algebraic Processes*, Prentice-Hall, New Jersey, (1963).

PROBLEMS

(**2.1**) Express the following numbers without fractions as (a) decimal numbers (b) binary numbers:

$$1/64, \quad 1/100, \quad 3/8, \quad 2/3, \quad 4/7$$

For example, in binary, $5/2$ gives $101/10$ which becomes 10.1.

(**2.2**) Express the following fixed point decimal numbers as floating point decimal numbers:

$$10736.2, \quad 2.7183, \quad 0.000001, \quad 0.7036$$

(**2.3**) Express the following floating point decimal numbers as fixed point decimal numbers:

$$0.1706 \text{ E3}, \quad 0.80375 \text{ E0}, \quad 0.38 \text{ E}-5, \quad 0.1416 \text{ E}-2$$

(**2.4**) Round the following numbers to (a) 3 decimal places, (b) 4 significant figures:

$$13.5055, \quad 1135.414736, \quad 0.0075005, \quad 3.14159, \quad 0.142857$$

(**2.5**) Propose a set of rules for rounding binary numbers, and apply them to round the following numbers to (a) 1 binary place, (b) 3 significant binary figures:

$$1111.101, \quad 10.11, \quad 0.1011 \text{ E3}$$

(**2.6**) Perform the following arithmetic operations and round each result to 4 significant figures:

$$107.4 + 0.01617, \quad 17.26 - 17.08, \quad 17.27 \times 15.16,$$
$$0.1514 \text{ E2} \div 0.2763 \text{ E5}$$

(**2.7**) For each of the results in Problem (2.6), calculate the rounding error to one significant figure measured as (a) an absolute error, (b) a relative error, (c) a percentage error.

(**2.8**) Calculate to 2 significant figures using a desk calculator (a) the absolute error, (b) the relative error, and (c) the percentage error in the following approximations:

$$\pi = 22/7, \quad \sqrt{2} = 1.414, \quad e = 2.7183$$

(**2.9**) Test the conditioning of the following problems, by making one per cent changes in the data on the left hand sides and observing the consequent percentage changes in the solution:

(i) $1.0x_1 + 0.50x_2 = 1.5$ (ii) $1.7 = x^{0.01}$
$ 0.50x_1 + 0.33x_2 = 0.83$

(**2.10**) Obtain formulae in terms of n for the truncation errors in the following n-step calculations, and evaluate these formulae for $n = 10$.

(i) Calculate an approximation to 2 from the sum

$$1 + 2^{-1} + 2^{-2} + 2^{-3} + \cdots + 2^{-n}$$

(ii) Calculate an approximation x_n to 1 from the recurrence

$$10x_i - 11x_{i-1} + x_{i-2} = 0 \qquad (i = 2, 3, 4, \ldots, n)$$

where $x_0 = 2$, $x_1 = 1.1$.
Hint: $x_i = A(t_1)^i + B(t_2)^i$, where t_1 and t_2 are roots of
$10t^2 - 11t + 1 = 0$

(2.11) Show that the calculation of x_n from the recurrence relation below is unstable, and explain why.

$$x_i = 49x_{i-1} + 50x_{i-2} \qquad (i = 2, 3, 4, \ldots)$$

where $x_0 = 1.001$, $x_1 = -1$.
Hint: Calculate x_4 exactly, and then repeat the calculation using 3 significant figure arithmetic.

(2.12) If $y'(x)$ is calculated approximately from the formula

$$[y(x + h) - y(x)]/h$$

for a chosen small value of h, what type(s) of error occur? Test this method with 4 significant figure arithmetic for $y = x^{1/4}$, with $x = 1$ and $h = 0.5, 0.1, 0.05, 0.01, 0.001$.

(2.13) Solve the following quadratic equation using 3 significant figure arithmetic to obtain values of x correct to 3 significant figures:

$$x^2 + 1000x + 10 = 0$$

(2.14) Solve the following quadratic equation using 3 significant figure arithmetic:

$$x^2 + 1.21x + 0.364 = 0$$

How many significant figures are needed for the calculations inside the square root to obtain solutions correct to 2 significant figures?

Chapter 3
Elementary mathematical calculations

ESSENTIAL THEORY

This chapter has two particular aims: to provide introductory examples of BASIC programming, and to cover various elementary mathematical calculations. These calculations are important in their own right, as well as being useful subsequently. A number of related programming exercises are included as problems at the end of the chapter.

In general small letters (e.g. x_i) will be used for the variables in the mathematics, and corresponding large letters (e.g. X(I)) will be used for the same variables in BASIC programs.

3.1 A product of numbers

It is often necessary to calculate a product such as

$$p = \prod_{i=1}^{n} x_i = x_1 x_2 \ldots x_n$$

where $x_1, x_2, \ldots, x_n$ are numbers specified as data. This is easily achieved in BASIC by setting the variable P equal to 1 and then successively multiplying it by X(1), X(2), . . . , X(N) as follows:

```
 60  P = 1
 70  FOR I = 1 TO N
 90  P = P * X(I)
100  NEXT I
```

A complete BASIC Program 3.1A is given below which incorporates this code. It is an *interactive* program in which the necessary data is called for at the terminal in response to INPUT statements. A second Program 3.1B is then given, which is a *batch* program and includes its own data in DATA statements.

In the remainder of the book, we shall generally provide interactive programs, since they are simple to use. However, the two programs below illustrate the way in which interactive programs may be modified into batch programs if need be. Note that, since a batch program includes its own data, DATA statements must be amended when any new set of data is required.

More complicated products may easily be programmed. For example, to calculate

$$\prod_{i=1}^{n} \frac{x_i^2}{1 - x_i} = \frac{x_1^2}{1 - x_1} \cdot \frac{x_2^2}{1 - x_2} \cdots \frac{x_n^2}{1 - x_n}$$

it is only necessary to change statement 90 in Program 3.1A into

90 P = P * X(I)*X(I)/(1 − X(I))

Program 3.1A TEST 1A: Product of terms (interactive program)

```
LIST
TEST1A

10      REM: TEST1A (INTERACTIVE) - PRODUCT OF X(1),...,X(N)
20      DIM X(50)
30      PRINT "NUMBER OF ITEMS";
40      INPUT N
50      PRINT "LIST OF ITEMS (1 PER LINE)"
60      P=1
70      FOR I=1 TO N
80      INPUT X(I)
90      P=P*X(I)
100     NEXT I
110     PRINT "PRODUCT:";P
120     END

Ready

RUN
TEST1A

NUMBER OF ITEMS? 5
LIST OF ITEMS (1 PER LINE)
? 1
? 2
? 3
? 4
? 5
PRODUCT: 120
Ready
```

Program 3.1B TEST 1B: Product of terms (batch program)

```
LIST
TEST1B

10      REM: TEST1B (BATCH) - PRODUCT OF X(1),...,X(N)
20      DIM X(50)
30      READ N
40      PRINT "NUMBER OF ITEMS:";N
50      PRINT "LIST OF ITEMS (1 PER LINE)"
60      P=1
70      FOR I=1 TO N
80      READ X(I)
90      PRINT X(I)
100     P=P*X(I)
110     NEXT I
120     PRINT "PRODUCT:";P
130     DATA 5
140     DATA 1,2,3,4,5
150     END

Ready
```

```
RUN
TEST1B

NUMBER OF ITEMS: 5
LIST OF ITEMS (1 PER LINE)
 1
 2
 3
 4
 5
PRODUCT: 120
Ready
```

3.2 A sum of numbers

The calculation of a sum

$$s = \sum_{i=1}^{n} x_i = x_1 + x_2 + \cdots + x_n$$

may be performed in exactly the same way as a product, except that multiplication is replaced by addition and s is initialised as 0 (where p was initialised as 1). Program 3.2 below incorporates the appropriate amendments to Program 3.1A. More complicated sums may easily be determined by amending statement 90, or by using Program 3.3 in the next section.

Program 3.2 TEST 2: Sum of terms

```
LIST
TEST2

10      REM: TEST2 - SUM OF X(1),...,X(N)
20      DIM X(50)
30      PRINT "NUMBER OF ITEMS";
40      INPUT N
50      PRINT "LIST OF ITEMS (1 PER LINE)"
60      S=0
70      FOR I=1 TO N
80      INPUT X(I)
90      S=S+X(I)
100     NEXT I
110     PRINT "SUM:";S
120     END

Ready

RUN
TEST2

NUMBER OF ITEMS? 5
LIST OF ITEMS (1 PER LINE)
? 1
? 34
? 23
? 68
? 2
SUM: 128
Ready
```

3.3 The sum of a series

A series in mathematics is the sum of a number of terms, which normally have values in some kind of numerical or algebraic pattern. The series may have a finite or infinite number of terms, and in the latter case we can only sum the infinite series if it is convergent. For example, the base of natural logarithms is given by the convergent series

$$e = 1 + \frac{1}{1!} + \frac{1}{2!} + \frac{1}{3!} + \cdots \qquad (3.1)$$

which may be calculated approximately by truncating the series after the term $1/n!$ for an appropriate choice of n. The general form of a (truncated) series of $(n + 1)$ terms is

$$s_n = a_0 + a_1 + a_2 + \cdots + a_i + \cdots + a_n \qquad (3.2)$$

In writing a BASIC program it is rather convenient to make use of the ratio of two consecutive terms

$$r_i = a_i/a_{i-1}$$

expressed in terms of i. This ratio is also relevant in an analysis of the series, since the *ratio test*[1] tells us that the series is convergent if

$$\lim_{i \to \infty} |r_i| < 1$$

If a_0 and $r_1, r_2, \ldots, r_n$ are specified, then the series (3.2) is given by

$$s_n = a_0\left(1 + \frac{a_1}{a_0} + \frac{a_1}{a_0} \cdot \frac{a_2}{a_1} + \cdots + \frac{a_1}{a_0} \cdot \frac{a_2}{a_1} \cdots \frac{a_n}{a_{n-1}}\right)$$

$$= a_0(1 + r_1 + r_1 r_2 + r_1 r_2 r_3 + \cdots + r_1 r_2 \cdots r_n)$$

The series may therefore be calculated by 'nested multiplication' in the form

$$s_n = a_0(1 + r_1(1 + r_2(1 + \cdots + r_{n-1}(1 + r_n(1)) \cdots))) \qquad (3.3)$$

An appropriate BASIC code is as follows:

```
 80  S = 1
 90  FOR I = N TO 0 STEP -1
100  S = 1 + R(I)*S
110  NEXT I
120  S = S * A(0)
```

The actual formula for R(I) (i.e. r_i) may be inserted in place of R(I) in statement 100. However, it is neater to specify R(I) by a DEF statement, since this enables a program to be written which is easily modified for a new series. In that case the following amendment is needed.

```
100  S = 1 + FNR(I)*S
```

and the following additional statement is required

140 DEF FNR(X) = [formula for r_x].

(Here X is a 'dummy variable', and any other variable name may be used in place of X.) An appropriate expression is inserted on the right of the equals sign in 140. For the series (3.1), for example,

$$r_i = \frac{a_i}{a_{i-1}} = \frac{1}{(i)!} \div \frac{1}{(i-1)!} = \frac{1}{i}$$

and so we may either use the single statement

100 S = 1 + S/I

or the pair of statements

100 S = 1 + FNR(I) * S
140 DEF FNR(X) = 1/X

The latter pair is used in the following complete program:

Program 3.3 TEST 3: Sum of series

```
LIST
TEST3

10      REM: TEST3 - SUMS SERIES S=A(0)+...+A(N)
20      REM: A=A(0) IS INPUT ; FNR(I)=A(I)/A(I-1) IS DEFINED FUNCTION
30      DIM R(100)
40      PRINT "NO OF TERMS AFTER FIRST";
50      INPUT N
60      PRINT "FIRST TERM";
70      INPUT A(0)
80      S=1
90      FOR I=N TO 1 STEP -1
100     S=1+FNR(I)*S
110     NEXT I
120     S=S*A(0)
130     PRINT "SUM:";S
140     DEF FNR(X)=1/X
150     END

Ready

RUN
TEST3

NO OF TERMS AFTER FIRST? 10
FIRST TERM? 1
SUM: 2.71828
Ready
```

Program notes

(1) To sum a new series, with ratios r_i, amend the definition of FNR(I) in instruction 140. For example, the series $1 + 2 + 3 + \cdots + 100$ may be summed by inputting N = 99, A(0) = 1, and using the definition:

140 DEF FNR(X) = (X + 1)/X

3.4 Processing lists of numbers

It is often necessary to pick out the largest or smallest of a set of numbers, or to list the numbers in ascending or descending order. To find the largest of $x_1, x_2, \ldots, x_n$, it is simply a matter of finding the larger of x_1 and x_2, then the larger of this number and x_3, and so on up to x_n. The following routine ends with this maximum value stored in the variable A.

```
10  A = X(1)
20  FOR I = 2 TO N
30  IF A > X(I) THEN 50
40  A = X(I)
50  NEXT I
```

The largest in *magnitude* of a set of numbers $x_1, \ldots, x_n$ may be obtained similarly by replacing A by ABS(A) and X(I) by ABS(X(I)) in the single line 30 of the above code. The smallest number is found in an analogous way and the reader is left to program this as an exercise (Problem 5).

More generally, if we wish to list the values of $x_1, \ldots, x_n$ in ascending order, then a simple procedure is to work through the current list (starting with $x_1, \ldots, x_n$ in that order) interchanging neighbouring pairs which are out of order, and then to repeat the whole procedure as often as necessary. In fact at most $n - 1$ cycles are needed (to move x_n from the last position to first position if necessary), and the following example illustrates the idea.

Initial List	Cycle 1				Cycle 2			Cycle 3		Cycle 4
$x_1 = 5$	4	4	4	4	3	3	3	2	2	1
$x_2 = 4$	5	3	3	3	4	2	2	3	1	2
$x_3 = 3$	3	5	2	2	2	4	1	1	3	3
$x_4 = 2$	2	2	5	1	1	1	4	4	4	4
$x_5 = 1$	1	1	1	5	5	5	5	5	5	5

In order to code the process, we must first code the interchange of two subscripted variables X(J) and X(K). There are right and wrong ways of doing this. The reader is left to deduce why an extra variable A must be used!

Correct code	Incorrect code
10 A = X(J)	10 X(K) = X(J)
20 X(J) = X(K)	20 X(J) = X(K)
30 X(K) = A	

The complete program for listing $x_1, \ldots, x_n$ in ascending order is given as Program 3.4 below. Note that the code for performing cycle I of the process consists of instructions 100 to 150, in which two adjacent numbers $X(J)$ and $X(J + 1)$ are interchanged if $X(J) \geq X(J + 1)$. The counter J runs through each element $X(J)$ in the list, and clearly this can take any value from 1 to $N - 1$.

Program 3.4 TEST 4: Reordering a list

```
LIST
TEST4

10      REM: TEST4 - LIST X(1),...,X(N) IN ASCENDING ORDER
20      DIM X(100)
30      PRINT "NO OF DATA";
40      INPUT N
50      PRINT "LIST OF DATA (1 PER LINE)"
60      FOR I=1 TO N
70      INPUT X(I)
80      NEXT I
90      FOR I=1 TO N-1
100     FOR J=1 TO N-1
110     IF X(J+1) > X(J) THEN 150
120     A=X(J)
130     X(J)=X(J+1)
140     X(J+1)=A
150     NEXT J
160     NEXT I
170     PRINT "SORTED DATA:"
180     FOR I=1 TO N
190     PRINT X(I)
200     NEXT I
210     END

Ready

RUN
TEST4

NO OF DATA? 5
LIST OF DATA (1 PER LINE)
? 5
? 1
? 4
? 3
? 2
SORTED DATA:
 1
 2
 3
 4
 5
Ready
```

3.5 Evaluation of a polynomial and its derivative (Horner's rule)

One of the most commonly occurring functions in mathematics is the polynomial

$$p_n(x) = a_0x^n + a_1x^{n-1} + \cdots + a_n \tag{3.4}$$

where $a_0, a_1, \ldots, a_n$ are some specified (constant) coefficients. It is often necessary to evaluate $p_n(x)$ for a given x, and indeed we may also require the value of its derivative

$$q_{n-1}(x) = p_n{}'(x) = na_0x^{n-1} + (n - 1)a_1x^{n-2} + \cdots + a_{n-1}$$

(and even perhaps the values of its 2nd, 3rd, ... derivatives). For example, Newton's method (see Chapter 4) for determining a zero of a polynomial $p_n(x)$ requires values of $p_n(x)$ and $p_n'(x)$ for various values of x.

The most efficient evaluation of (3.4) uses nested multiplication (compare the series summation (3.3) of Section 3.3) as follows:

$$p_n = a_n + x(a_{n-1} + x(a_{n-2} + x(\cdots + xa_0)\cdots)) \qquad (3.5)$$

In particular note that the form (3.5) involves only n multiplications altogether, whereas (3.4) requires $n - 1$ multiplications to determine $x^2, x^3, \ldots, x^n$ plus n further multiplications (by $a_0, \ldots, a_{n-1}$). The algebraic sequence of calculations in (3.5) may be written

$$p_0 = a_0, p_1 = xp_0 + a_1, p_2 = xp_1 + a_2, \ldots, p_n = xp_{n-1} + a_n$$

where $p_0, p_1, \ldots, p_{n-1}$ are results of intermediate calculations. In summary

$$p_0 = a_0, p_i = xp_{i-1} + a_i \qquad (i = 1, \ldots, n) \qquad (3.6)$$

and this 'recurrence' is called 'Horner's rule' for evaluating the polynomial. Differentiating (3.6):

$$(p_0' = 0), p_1' = p_0, \ p_i' = xp_{i-1}' + p_{i-1} \qquad (i = 2, \ldots, n)$$

i.e. $\qquad q_0 = p_0, q_i = xq_{i-1} + p_i \qquad (i = 1, \ldots, n-1) \qquad (3.7)$

where $q_i = p_{i+1}'$ and in particular $q_{n-1} = p_n'$.

Thus, to evaluate $p_n(x)$ and its derivative $q_{n-1}(x)$, we need only specify x and perform the two recurrences (3.6) and (3.7), and this is done in the Program 3.5 below. Note that all subscripts may be dropped from the variables p and q, since only the last values p_n and q_{n-1} are required. The identity

$$p_i = xp_{i-1} + a_i$$

is achieved automatically by the assignment statement

$$P = X*P + A(I).$$

Program 3.5 TEST 5: Polynomial and its derivative

```
LIST
TEST5

10      REM: TEST5 - CALC P=A(0)*X^N+...+A(N) AND Q=P'
20      DIM A(20),P(20),Q(20)
30      PRINT "DEGREE";
40      INPUT N
50      PRINT "COEFFICIENTS (1 PER LINE)"
60      FOR I=0 TO N
70      INPUT A(I)
80      NEXT I
90      PRINT "X VALUE";
```

```
100      INPUT X
110      P=A(0)
120      Q=P
130      FOR I=1 TO N
140      P=X*P+A(I)
150      IF I=N THEN 170
160      Q=X*Q+P
170      NEXT I
180      PRINT "POLYNOMIAL:";P
190      PRINT "DERIVATIVE:";Q
200      END

Ready

RUN
TEST5

DEGREE? 3
COEFFICIENTS (1 PER LINE)
? 1
? 2
? 3
? 4
X VALUE? .5
POLYNOMIAL: 6.125
DERIVATIVE: 5.75
Ready
```

3.6 Limits of ratios

A BASIC program can also be written to investigate a limit such as

$$\text{(i)} \ \lim_{x \to 0} \frac{\sin x}{x}, \quad \text{(ii)} \ \lim_{x \to 0} \frac{1 - \cos x}{x^2}, \quad \text{(iii)} \ \lim_{x \to 0} \frac{1 - \cos x}{1 - \cosh x}$$

where $\cosh x = \frac{1}{2}(e^x + e^{-x})$.

Although mathematical methods, based on Taylor series or l'Hopitâl's rule[1], may easily be applied to deduce the values 1, $\frac{1}{2}$, and -1 for these respective limits, it is instructive to calculate the values of these quotients for successively smaller choices of x and deduce the limiting values by inspection. However, note that very small values of x must be avoided, since a computer cannot ultimately divide zero by zero. Moreover a term like $1 - \cos x$ or $1 - \cosh x$ is subject to very large significance error as $x \to 0$, and so we may obtain very inaccurate values of the ratio if x is taken too small (before reaching the stage of dividing 0 by 0).

These points show up rather clearly in the tests of Program 3.6 below. In particular for (ii), the ratio $(1 - \cos x)/x^2$ is given the accurate value of .499 for $x = .01$, it takes the 'meaningless' value of .42 for $x = .001$ (due to significance error), and the numerator becomes zero (by rounding) for $x = .0001$.

Program 3.6 below calculates the approximate limit as $x \to 0$ of the quotient of any two functions $f(x)$ and $g(x)$, specified by DEF statements, and it is tested on each of the three examples above.

Program 3.6 TEST 6: Limit of ratio of functions

```
LIST


TEST6

10 REM- TEST6: LIMIT OF F(X)/G(X) AS X APPROACHES 0
20 PRINT "NO OF DECIMALS TO WHICH X =0 ";
30 INPUT N
40 X=1
50 PRINT "X:","F/G :"
60 I=0
70 R=FNF(X)/FNG(X)
80 PRINT X,R
90 X=.1*X
100 I=I+1
110 IF I<=N THEN 70
120 DEF FNF(X)=SIN(X)
130 DEF FNG(X)=X
140 END

READY

RUN


TEST6

NO OF DECIMALS TO WHICH X =0 ? 4
X:              F/G :
 1              .841471
 .1             .998334
 .01            .999983
 1.00000E-03    1
 1.00000E-04    1

READY

120 DEF FNF(X)=1-COS(X)
130 DEF FNG(X)=X*X
RUN


TEST6

NO OF DECIMALS TO WHICH X =0 ? 4
X:              F/G :
 1              .459698
 .1             .49957
 .01            .498891
 1.00000E-03    .417233
 1.00000E-04    0

READY

120 DEF FNF(X)=1-COS(X)
130 DEF FNG(X)=1-.5*(EXP(X)+EXP(-X))
RUN


TEST6

NO OF DECIMALS TO WHICH X =0 ? 4
X:              F/G :
 1              -.846463
 .1             -.998309
 .01            -.998807
 1.00000E-03    -.875
 1.00000E-04    0

READY
```

3.7 Two simultaneous linear equations – integer coefficients

One of the earliest algebraic problems we encounter is that of finding the values of a pair of unknowns x_1, x_2 given by a pair of simultaneous linear equations

$$a_{11}x_1 + a_{12}x_2 = b_1 \atop a_{21}x_1 + a_{22}x_2 = b_2 \Bigg\}$$ (3.8)

where a_{11}, a_{12}, a_{21}, a_{22}, b_1, b_2 are given numbers, called the coefficients. The numbering of these coefficients with suffices is commonly used in connection with matrices[2], since (3.8) can be rewritten as

$$\mathbf{Ax = b}, \quad \text{where} \quad \mathbf{A} = \begin{pmatrix} a_{11} & a_{12} \\ a_{21} & a_{22} \end{pmatrix}, \quad \mathbf{x} = \begin{pmatrix} x_1 \\ x_2 \end{pmatrix}, \quad \mathbf{b} = \begin{pmatrix} b_1 \\ b_2 \end{pmatrix}.$$

The following assumptions will be made to simplify the problem (by eliminating most of the rounding errors) and make it relatively easy to program in BASIC.

Assumptions:

(i) All coefficients $a_{11}, \ldots, b_2$ are integers.
(ii) All coefficients have absolute values less than 10^8.
(iii) None of the left hand side coefficients $a_{11}, a_{12}, a_{21}, a_{22}$ are zero.

With these assumptions, the calculations of c_1, c_2, and d below in BASIC are performed exactly, numbers do not approach the limits of the computer's capacity, and it is easy to characterise the nature of the solution (unique, non-existent, or many-valued).

By eliminating first x_2 and then x_1, we deduce that

$$x_1 \cdot d = c_1 \quad \text{and} \quad x_2 \cdot d = -c_2$$ (3.9)

where $c_1 = b_1 a_{22} - b_2 a_{12}$, $c_2 = b_1 a_{21} - b_2 a_{11}$, $d = a_{11}a_{22} - a_{12}a_{21}$. The solution is therefore unique provided that $d \neq 0$. In the case $d = 0$, it follows from (3.9) that $c_1 = c_2 = 0$, or else there are no solutions. When $d = 0$ and $c_1 = c_2 = 0$, then

$$\frac{a_{21}}{a_{11}}(a_{11}x_1 + a_{12}x_2 - b_1) = (a_{21}x_1 + a_{22}x_2 - b_2)$$

and so the two equations (3.8) reduce to one equation. There are then many solutions, and so we may choose x_1 arbitrarily and define x_2 from it (or vice-versa). In summary, noting that $c_1 = c_2 = 0$ is equivalent to one condition $c_1^2 + c_2^2 = 0$, the cases are:

(i) If $d \neq 0$, there is a unique solution $x_1 = c_1/d$, $x_2 = -c_2/d$.
(ii) If $d = 0$ and $c_1^2 + c_2^2 \neq 0$, then there is no solution.
(iii) If $d = 0$ and $c_1^2 + c_2^2 = 0$, then $x_1 = C$,
   $x_2 = (b_1 - a_{11}C)/a_{12}$ where C is an arbitrary constant.

The following BASIC Program 3.7 incorporates these three cases by way of three branches, starting at instructions 110, 150, and 190, respectively. The following three pairs of simultaneous equations are tested in the sample runs:

(i) $\begin{aligned} x_1 + 2x_2 &= 5 \\ 3x_1 + 4x_2 &= 6 \end{aligned}$ (ii) $\begin{aligned} x_1 + 2x_2 &= 5 \\ 2x_1 + 4x_2 &= 10 \end{aligned}$ (iii) $\begin{aligned} x_1 + 2x_2 &= 5 \\ 2x_1 + 4x_2 &= 6 \end{aligned}$

Program 3.7 TEST 7: Simultaneous equations

```
LIST


TEST7

10 REM- TEST7: 2 SIMULTANEOUS LINEAR EQUATIONS WITH
20 REM- INTEGER COEFFICIENTS, NON-ZERO L.H.S. COEFFICIENTS.
25 DIM A(2,2),X(2),B(2)
30 PRINT "L.H.S. COEFFICIENTS (INPUT ON ONE LINE)"
40 INPUT A(1,1),A(1,2),A(2,1),A(2,2)
50 PRINT "R.H.S. COEFFICIENTS (ON ONE LINE)"
60 INPUT B(1),B(2)
70 C1=B(1)*A(2,2)-B(2)*A(1,2)
80 C2=B(1)*A(2,1)-B(2)*A(1,1)
90 D=A(1,1)*A(2,2)-A(1,2)*A(2,1)
100 IF D=0 THEN 150
110 X(1)=C1/D
120 X(2)=-C2/D
130 PRINT "UNIQUE SOLN X1,X2=";X(1);",";X(2)
140 GO TO 220
150 E=C1*C1+C2*C2
160 IF E=0 THEN 190
170 PRINT "NO SOLUTIONS X1,X2"
180 GO TO 220
190 E=B(1)/A(1,2)
200 F=-A(1,1)/A(1,2)
210 PRINT "X1=C (ARBITRARY),   X2=";E;"+C*";F
220 END

READY



RUN


TEST7

L.H.S. COEFFICIENTS (INPUT ON ONE LINE)
? 1,2,3,4
R.H.S. COEFFICIENTS (ON ONE LINE)
? 5,6
UNIQUE SOLN X1,X2=-4 , 4.5

READY




RUN


TEST7

L.H.S. COEFFICIENTS (INPUT ON ONE LINE)
? 1,2,2,4
R.H.S. COEFFICIENTS (ON ONE LINE)
? 5,10
X1=C (ARBITRARY),   X2= 2.5 +C*-.5

READY
```

```
RUN

TEST7

L.H.S. COEFFICIENTS (INPUT ON ONE LINE)
? 1,2,2,4
R.H.S. COEFFICIENTS (ON ONE LINE)
? 5,6
NO SOLUTIONS X1,X2

READY
```

If we wish to remove the restriction that $a_{11}, a_{12}, a_{21}, a_{22}$ should not be zero, then no less than seven branches have to be included in the BASIC program! A flow chart which details these seven separate cases is given in Figure 3.1. The reader is invited to write such a program, and this appears as Problem 8 at the end of the Chapter.

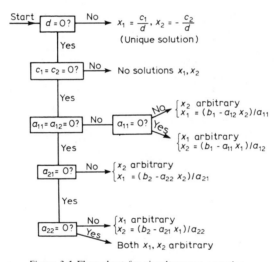

Figure 3.1 Flow chart for simultaneous equations

3.8 Quadratic equations

In Chapter 2 we saw that there were two particular practical difficulties in obtaining the solutions $x = x_1$ and $x = x_2$ of a quadratic equation

$$ax^2 + bx + c = 0 \qquad (3.10)$$

where a, b, c are given (decimal) numbers with $a \neq 0$. Firstly, the problem may be ill-conditioned, as in Equation (2.6). However, there is little that can be done about this, other than to be aware of the dangers. Secondly, significance error may adversely affect the results if we use the standard formula for the roots x_1, x_2:

$$x_1, x_2 = (-b_1 \pm \sqrt{d})/a \qquad (3.11)$$

where $b_1 = b/2$ and $d = b_1^2 - ac$, as in the case of (2.13). Good results can, however, be assured when ac is small compared with b_1^2, by using the formula

$$x_1 x_2 = c/a$$

to calculate x_2 from x_1. Here the sign of $\sqrt{d}$ which defines x_1 is taken to be $+$ if b is negative and $-$ if b is positive, so that there is no cancellation in the numerator of (3.11) in calculating x_1.

Another point to note is that if d is negative then (3.10) has a pair of complex roots. There are therefore three cases in all to consider, and the algorithm for solving (3.10) is as follows.

Algorithm 3.8 Quadratic equation

   (i) For $d \geqslant 0, b \geqslant 0$: $x_1 = (-b_1 - \sqrt{d})/a, x_2 = c/(ax_1)$
  (ii) For $d \geqslant 0, b < 0$: $x_1 = (-b_1 + \sqrt{d})/a, x_2 = c/(ax_1)$
 (iii) For $d < 0$: $x_1, x_2 = u \pm iv$ where $u = -b_1/a, v = \sqrt{(-d)}/a$.

The BASIC program to perform Algorithm 3.8 is as follows.

Program 3.8 TEST 8: Quadratic equations

```
LIST


TEST8

10 REM- TEST8: SOLVES THE QUADRATIC EQUATION A*X*X +B*X +C =0
20 PRINT 'QUADRATIC EQN COEFFICIENTS A,B,C';
30 INPUT A,B,C
40 IF A=0 GO TO 290
50 B1=.5*B
60 D=B1*B1-A*C
70 IF D<0 GO TO 190
80 REM-  TWO REAL ROOTS CALCULATED
90 E=SQR(D)
100 IF B<0 GO TO 130
110 X1=(-B1-E)/A
120 GO TO 140
130 X1=(-B1+E)/A
140 X2=C/(A*X1)
150 PRINT 'REAL ROOTS'
160 PRINT 'X1,X2 =';X1;',';X2
170 GO TO 310
180 REM- COMPLEX ROOTS FOUND'
190 E=SQR(-D)
200 U1=-B1/A
210 U2=U1
220 V1=E/A
230 V2=-V1
240 PRINT 'COMPLEX ROOTS U+I*V , U-I*V'
250 PRINT 'REAL PART U :','IMAG PART V :'
260 PRINT U1,V1
270 PRINT U2,V2
280 GO TO 310
290 PRINT 'LEADING COEFFICIENT IS ZERO'
300 PRINT 'NOT QUADRATIC'
310 END

READY
```

```
RUN

TEST8

QUADRATIC EQN COEFFICIENTS A,B,C? 10,7,-12
REAL ROOTS
X1,X2 =-1.5 , .8

READY




RUN

TEST8

QUADRATIC EQN COEFFICIENTS A,B,C? 1,-50,1
REAL ROOTS
X1,X2 = 49.98 , .020008

READY




RUN

TEST8

QUADRATIC EQN COEFFICIENTS A,B,C? 1,1,1
COMPLEX ROOTS U+I*V , U-I*V
REAL PART U : IMAG PART V :
-.5           .866025
-.5          -.866025

READY
```

3.9 Three-term recurrence relations

A three-term recurrence relation takes the form

$$a_i x_i + b_i x_{i-1} + c_i x_{i-2} = 0 \qquad (i = 2, 3, 4, \ldots) \qquad (3.12)$$

and requires two initial conditions of the form

$$x_0 = u, \quad x_1 = v \qquad (3.13)$$

where a_i, b_i, c_i, u, v are all specified constants.

The formulae (3.12) and (3.13) define a sequence of values x_0, x_1, $x_2, \ldots, x_i, \ldots$ uniquely. Such recurrence relations occur commonly in practice, two occurrences being in finite difference methods for ordinary differential equations and in numerical methods for polynomial equations.

An efficient *numerical* method for solving (3.12), (3.13) simply consists of specifying x_0, x_1 by (3.13) and then successively calculating

$$x_i = -(b_i x_{i-1} + c_i x_{i-2})/a_i \qquad (i = 2, 3, 4, \ldots) \qquad (3.14)$$

The only note of caution here is that (3.14) may be numerically unstable (see Equation (2.11) and Table 2.3).

An elegant *mathematical* method may also be found, which is less efficient than (3.14) but which provides an explicit solution. Suppose in particular that $a_i = a, b_i = b, c_i = c$, so that these coefficients have the same values for every i. Then solve the quadratic equation

$$at^2 + bt + c = 0 \tag{3.15}$$

giving

$$t_1, t_2 = [-b \pm \sqrt{(b^2 - 4ac)}]/(2a)$$

It follows that

$$x_i = A(t_1)^i + B(t_2)^i \tag{3.16}$$

where A and B are certain constants. Applying (3.13)

$$x_0 = u = A + B, \qquad x_1 = v = At_1 + Bt_2$$

and hence

$$A = \frac{t_2 u - v}{t_2 - t_1} \quad \text{and} \quad B = \frac{t_1 u - v}{t_1 - t_2} \tag{3.17}$$

Thus x_i is given explicitly by (3.16) and (3.17).

A simple and interesting problem which illustrates recurrence relations is the following one. A ring is divided into n arcs, and it is required to paint each arc with one of a set of k different colours, so that no two adjacent arcs have the same colour. In how many ways can this be done? Let x_n be the number of ways. Also suppose that y_n is the number of ways of painting n arcs, when it is required that the first and last should have the *same* colour. Then the sum $x_n + y_n$ is the number of ways of painting n arcs when the colours of the first and last are of no consequence. It is hence easy to deduce (and this is left as an exercise to the reader) that

$$y_i = x_{i-1}$$

and

$$(x_i + y_i) = (k - 1)(x_{i-1} + y_{i-1}) \tag{3.18}$$

where $x_1 = 0$, $y_1 = k$. Eliminating y_i and y_{i-1} from (3.18):

$$x_i - (k - 2)x_{i-1} - (k - 1)x_{i-2} = 0 \tag{3.19}$$

where

$$x_0 = k, \qquad x_1 = 0. \tag{3.20}$$

We therefore have a recurrence relation, with coefficients independent of i. We may then calculate x_i efficiently from (3.14) using the constants $a_i = 1$, $b_i = -(k - 2)$, $c_i = -(k - 1)$, $u = k$, $v = 0$. Alternatively (3.16) and (3.17) give

$$x_i = A(-1)^i + B(k - 1)^i$$

where

$$A = \frac{(k - 1)k + 0}{(k - 1) - (-1)} = k - 1$$

and

$$B = \frac{(-1)k + 0}{-1 - (k - 1)} = 1$$

Hence

$$x_i = (k - 1)(-1)^i + (k - 1)^i$$

In the particular case $k = 3$, for example, the constants are

$$a = 1, \quad b = -1, \quad c = -2, \quad u = 3, \quad v = 1$$

and the solution is

$$x_i = 2(-1)^i + (2)^i$$

i.e. $x_0, x_1, x_2, x_3, \ldots = 3, 0, 6, 6, \ldots$.

The following program, Program 3.9, solves (3.12) for constant values a, b, c of a_i, b_i, c_i, using Equation (3.14). It is tested for the Equations (3.19), (3.20) with $k = 3$.

Program 3.9 TEST 9: Recurrence relation

```
LIST
TEST9

10      REM- TEST9: SOLVE A*X(I)+B*X(I-1)+C*X(I-2)=0 ; X(0),X(1) GIVEN.
20      DIM X(30)
30      PRINT "RECURRENCE COEFFICIENTS A,B,C";
40      INPUT A,B,C
50      PRINT "NUMBER OF RESULTS REQUIRED";
60      INPUT N
70      PRINT "INITIAL VALUES X(0),X(1)";
80      INPUT X(0),X(1)
90      B=-B/A
100     C=-C/A
110     PRINT "I:","X(I):"
120     FOR I=2 TO N
130     X(I)=B*X(I-1)+C*X(I-2)
140     PRINT I,X(I)
150     NEXT I
160     END

Ready
```

```
RUN
TEST9

RECURRENCE COEFFICIENTS A,B,C? 1,-1,-2
NUMBER OF RESULTS REQUIRED? 10
INITIAL VALUES X(0),X(1)? 3,0
I:              X(I):
  2               6
  3               6
  4              18
  5              30
  6              66
  7             126
  8             258
  9             510
 10            1026
Ready
```

3.10 Elementary matrix calculations

Matrices are a shorthand device for simplifying algebra[2] and so it is instructive to end this chapter with some elementary matrix operations. This will also provide a useful exercise in programming multiple loops. We shall determine the product of two matrices and the product of a matrix and a vector.

Suppose that **A** is a given $m \times n$ matrix (m rows and n columns) with elements a_{ij} (in row i and column j), and that **B** is another given $n \times p$ matrix with elements b_{ij}. Then the product

$$C = A \cdot B$$

is an $m \times p$ matrix with elements c_{ij} defined by

$$c_{ij} = \sum_{k=1}^{n} a_{ik} b_{kj} \qquad (i = 1, \ldots, m; j = 1, \ldots, p) \qquad (3.21)$$

In the particular case $p = 1$, **B** is in fact an $m \times 1$ vector (x say) and the product

$$y = Ax$$

is an $m \times 1$ vector, defined by (3.21) with

$$y_i = c_{i1} \quad \text{and} \quad b_{k1} = x_k$$

For example,

if $\qquad \mathbf{A} = \begin{pmatrix} 3 & 2 \\ 5 & -1 \\ 4 & 9 \end{pmatrix}$ and $\mathbf{B} = \begin{pmatrix} 1 & 5 & 7 & 2 \\ 4 & 8 & 1 & 6 \end{pmatrix}$

then $\mathbf{C} = \begin{pmatrix} 11 & 31 & 23 & 18 \\ 1 & 17 & 34 & 4 \\ 40 & 92 & 37 & 62 \end{pmatrix}$

and if

$$\mathbf{A} = \begin{pmatrix} 3 & 2 \\ 5 & -1 \\ 4 & 9 \end{pmatrix} \quad \text{and} \quad \mathbf{B} = \mathbf{x} = \begin{pmatrix} 1 \\ 4 \end{pmatrix} \quad \text{then} \quad \mathbf{C} = \mathbf{y} = \begin{pmatrix} 11 \\ 1 \\ 40 \end{pmatrix}$$

In a BASIC program c_{ij}, a_{ik}, b_{kj} are represented by variables with two subscripts: C(I, J), A(I, K), B(K, J). The relation (3.21) is defined with loops on i and j, and the sum is accumulated in a loop on k. The program, Program 3.10, is given below.

Program 3.10 TEST 10: Matrix product

```
LIST
TEST10

10     REM- TEST10: CALCULATES MATRIX PRODUCT A*B
20     DIM A(10,10),B(10,10),C(10,10)
30     PRINT "NO OF ROWS AND COLS IN A ";
40     INPUT M,N
50     PRINT "ELEMENTS OF A (1 PER LINE)"
60     FOR I=1 TO M
70     FOR J=1 TO N
80     INPUT A(I,J)
90     NEXT J
100    NEXT I
110    PRINT "NO OF ROWS AND COLS IN B ";
120    INPUT N1,P
130    IF N1=N THEN 160
140    PRINT "A AND B ARE INCOMPATIBLE"
150    GO TO 350
160    PRINT "ELEMENTS OF B (1 PER LINE)"
170    FOR I=1 TO N
180    FOR J=1 TO P
190    INPUT B(I,J)
200    NEXT J
210    NEXT I
220    PRINT "NO OF ROWS AND COLS IN C :";
230    PRINT M;P
240    PRINT "ELEMENTS OF C :"
250    FOR I=1 TO M
260    FOR J=1 TO P
270    D=0
280    FOR K=1 TO N
290    D=D+A(I,K)*B(K,J)
300    NEXT K
310    C(I,J)=D
320    PRINT C(I,J)
330    NEXT J
340    NEXT I
350    END

Ready

RUN
TEST10

NO OF ROWS AND COLS IN A ? 1,1
ELEMENTS OF A (1 PER LINE)
? 1
NO OF ROWS AND COLS IN B ? 2,2
A AND B ARE INCOMPATIBLE
Ready
```

```
RUN
TEST10

NO OF ROWS AND COLS IN A ? 3,2
ELEMENTS OF A (1 PER LINE)
? 3
? 2
? 5
? -1
? 4
? 9
NO OF ROWS AND COLS IN B ? 2,4
ELEMENTS OF B (1 PER LINE)
? 1
? 5
? 7
? 2
? 4
? 8
? 1
? 6
NO OF ROWS AND COLS IN C : 3   4
ELEMENTS OF C :
 11
 31
 23
 18
 1
 17
 34
 4
 40
 92
 37
 62
Ready
```

Program notes

(1) The elements a_{ij} and b_{ij} must be input one at a time on separate lines. There is no facility in BASIC for inputting arrays of elements set out in rows, except by using MAT INPUT statements.

(2) The elements c_{ij} of the product matrix are output one element per line working across each row in turn.

3.11 References

1. A.C. Bajpai, L.R. Mustoe, and D. Walker, *Engineering Mathematics*, Wiley, Chichester, (1974)
2. J.C. Mason, *BASIC Matrix Methods*, Butterworths, (1984)

PROBLEMS

(3.1) Modify Program 3.1A to calculate the expressions

$$\frac{n(n-1)\ldots(n-i+1)}{1.2\ldots i} \quad \text{for} \quad i = 0, 1, \ldots, n$$

where the integer n is specified as a datum. Calculate these expressions for $n = 5$, $n = 10$. How are such expressions used in mathematics?

(3.2) Modify Program 3.2 so that it calculates all of the following expressions

(i) $\sum_{i=1}^{n} x_i$ (ii) $\sum_{i=1}^{n} y_i$ (iii) $\sum_{i=1}^{n} x_i^2$ (iv) $\sum_{i=1}^{n} x_i y_i$

where x_i, y_i are data. Calculate these expressions when $x_i = i$, $y_i = i^2$ ($i = 1, \ldots, 10$).

(3.3) Determine the general terms a_i in each of the following infinite series, and hence calculate the sums of the series correct to 3 decimal places using Program 3.3.

(i) $1 - \dfrac{x^2}{2!} + \dfrac{x^4}{4!} - \dfrac{x^6}{6!} + \cdots$ (for $x = .01, .1$)

(ii) $x + \dfrac{x^3}{3!} + \dfrac{x^5}{5!} + \ldots$ (for $x = .01, .1$)

(iii) $x - \dfrac{x^2}{2} + \dfrac{x^3}{3} - \dfrac{x^4}{4} + \cdots$ (for $x = .1, .5$)

What functions do these series represent?

(3.4) Use Program 3.3 to calculate

(i) $1 + (\tfrac{1}{2})^2 + \left(\dfrac{1.3}{2.4}\right)^2 + \cdots + \left(\dfrac{1.3 \ldots 19}{2.4 \ldots 20}\right)^2$

(ii) $1 + \dfrac{10}{1} + \dfrac{10.9}{1.2} + \dfrac{10.9.8}{1.2.3} + \cdots + \dfrac{10.9 \ldots 1}{1.2 \ldots 10}$

Why does (ii) give 2^{10}?

(3.5) Write a program which inputs as data a set of N numbers $X(1), \ldots, X(N)$ and then (i) calculates the smallest of the numbers, (ii) calculates the smallest in magnitude of the numbers and (iii) prints out the numbers in descending order. Test this program on the data:

$$1, \quad 5, \quad 2, \quad -4, \quad -6, \quad 8, \quad 3, \quad -5, \quad 6, \quad -1.$$

(3.6) Modify Program 3.5 to evaluate a polynomial and its first two derivatives at a point x, and test this program on the data used in the Sample Run of Program 3.5.

(3.7) Determine mathematically the following limits as $x \to 0$:

$$\text{(i)} \quad \frac{x - \tan x}{x^3} \qquad \text{(ii)} \quad 10^x \qquad \text{(iii)} \quad \frac{x - \sin x}{x - \sinh x} \qquad \text{(iv)} \quad x^{-1}e^{-1/x}$$

Verify these results with Program 3.6.

(3.8) Write a *user-proof* program, based on the flowchart of Figure 3.1, to solve a pair of simultaneous equations with integer coefficients in which the coefficients on the left hand side may be zero.

(3.9) Test Program 3.8 on the quadratics (2.6) and (2.13) of Chapter 2. Construct a quadratic equation for which the significance error occurring in the evaluation of the square root is as large as possible (on your computer).

(3.10) Use Program 3.9 to calculate x_5 from the recurrence

$$x_i - 10.1x_{i-1} + x_{i-2} = 0$$

with
$$x_0 = 1, \quad x_1 = .1$$

Do you reproduce the true values? (See Table 2.3.) Repeat the calculation using all pairs of values of x_0 and x_1 that have relative errors of ± 0.1 per cent.

(3.11) Write a program which calculates the solution $\{x_i\}$ of the three-term recurrence relation

$$ax_i + bx_{i-1} + cx_{i-2} = 0$$

(i.e. (3.12) with coefficients independent of i) subject to (3.13), but which is based on the explicit formulae (3.16), (3.17) rather than on the assignment (3.14). Incorporate the relevant part of Program 3.8 to solve the quadratic equation (3.15), and input a, b, c, u, v as data.

(3.12) Write a program which calculates the solution $\{x_i\}$ of (3.12) subject to (3.13), where values of a_i, b_i, c_i vary with i and are specified by defined functions (of i) within the program.

Test the program (checking it by hand calculations) for the determination of x_5 from:

$$x_i = ix_{i-1} + x_{i-2}, \quad x_0 = 0, \quad x_1 = 1$$

(3.13) Write a program to calculate $\mathbf{A}^T\mathbf{A}$ from $\mathbf{A}$, and test it on the three matrices:

$$\mathbf{A} = \begin{pmatrix} 3 & 2 \\ 5 & -1 \\ 4 & 9 \end{pmatrix}, \quad \begin{pmatrix} 3 & 2 \\ 5 & -1 \end{pmatrix}, \quad \begin{pmatrix} 7 \\ 3 \end{pmatrix}, \quad \text{respectively.}$$

What properties does such a matrix have in general? ($\mathbf{A}^\mathrm{T}$ is the matrix whose rows are the columns of $\mathbf{A}$.)

Chapter 4

Nonlinear algebraic equations

ESSENTIAL THEORY

4.1 Introduction

In Chapter 3 (Section 3.8) we discussed the elementary problem of solving a quadratic equation, and a standard set of formulae were used for the solution. This problem is in fact the simplest example of a general problem frequently encountered in practice, namely the equation

$$f(x) = 0 \qquad (4.1)$$

where f is some specified algebraic function. Such an algebraic equation is called 'nonlinear' because, except for the trivial example $f(x) \equiv ax + b = 0$, where a and b are given constants, the function f does *not* satisfy a linear relationship of the form

$$f(c_1 x_1 + c_2 x_2) = c_1 f(x_1) + c_2 f(x_2)$$

Indeed such a relationship does not even hold for a quadratic.

Four simple examples of nonlinear algebraic equations of form (4.1) are

$$x^3 - x - 1 = 0 \qquad (4.2)$$

$$x^4 - 7x^3 + 1 = 0 \qquad (4.3)$$

$$\tan x - 2x = 0 \qquad (4.4)$$

and

$$e^{-x} - x = 0 \qquad (4.5)$$

Note also that any algebraic equation with both left and right hand sides, such as

$$x = \exp(-x^2)$$

can be rewritten in the form (4.1) simply by collecting terms on the left:

$$f(x) = x - \exp(-x^2) = 0 \qquad (4.6)$$

The first two equations (4.2) and (4.3), the cubic and the quartic equation, have the special property (in common with the quadratic equation) that their solution may be determined exactly by a finite set of formulae. However, Equations (4.4), (4.5), and (4.6) cannot be solved exactly in a finite number of steps, and indeed this is true for nonlinear algebraic equations in general. In this chapter we shall therefore look for methods of obtaining approximate rather than exact solutions. The basic approach is to start with an estimated value or range of values for the solution and then to determine a number of successively better approximations to the solution.

In Chapter 2 we discussed the different types of errors which occurred in a numerical method. Since all methods in this chapter are based on iterative or repetitive processes, which constantly test potential solutions of the given equation, we can neglect rounding error. So truncation error is the only form of error which is relevant here.

4.2 Existence of solutions

The first task in solving (4.1) is to determine a rough location for the required solution, and the standard way of achieving this is by inspecting the values of $f(x)$ at regular intervals and looking for changes of sign. For example the function (4.5), namely

$$f(x) = e^{-x} - x \tag{4.7}$$

is tabulated in Table 4.1 at intervals of 0.25 in $[0, 1]$, and it is clear that a solution must lie between 0.5 and 0.75. As illustrated in Figure 4.1, the graph of the continuous curve $y = f(x)$ has to cross the axis $y = 0$ somewhere between these two values.

Also, by considering the gradient of $y = f(x)$, it may be possible to guarantee that there is only one solution of $f(x) = 0$ between two particular x values. For example (4.7) has the gradient

$$\frac{dy}{dx} = f'(x) = - (e^{-x} + 1)$$

which is negative for all values of x. So in this case $f(x)$ decreases steadily between $x = 0.5$ and 0.75, and there is precisely one solution of the Equation (4.7) in this range.

Now that an interval $[a, b]$, say, has been found which contains the solution, we can go about the task of determining that solution accurately. There are two main types of methods for achieving

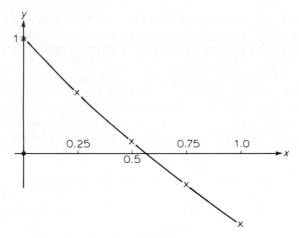

Figure 4.1 The function $y = f(x) = e^{-x} - x$

Table 4.1 Values of
$f(x) = e^{-x} - x$

x	$f(x)$
0	1
0.25	0.529
0.5	0.107
0.75	−0.278
1.00	−0.632

this, search methods and iteration methods. A simple but very effective search method is the 'bisection method'.

4.3 The bisection method

In the last section we established the existence of a solution by inspecting values of $f(x)$ and looking for a change of signs. In fact this process can be carried out repetitively so as to determine successively smaller intervals containing the solution. The simplest such method is the *bisection method* which proceeds as follows.

Consider example (4.7), with $[a, b] = [.5, .75]$. Here

$$f(.5) > 0, \quad f(.75) < 0$$

By evaluating f at the mid point .625, we find that $f(.625) < 0$ and hence the solution lies in the bisected interval $[.5, .625]$. Again by evaluating f at the mid point .5625 of this new interval, we find that $f(.5625) > 0$ and hence the solution lies in the (once again) bisected interval $[.5625, .625]$. Clearly these bisections can be continued as often as required to obtain an arbitrarily small interval containing the solution.

This method may be generalised as follows. Suppose that after i bisections the solution has been located in the interval $[a_i, b_i]$, where $[a_0, b_0]$ is the initial interval $[a, b]$. Then $f(a_i)$ and $f(b_i)$ have opposite signs. Now consider the mid point

$$c_i = \tfrac{1}{2}(a_i + b_i)$$

and calculate $f(c_i)$. Then there are two possibilities:

(i) $f(a_i)$ and $f(c_i)$ have opposite signs. $\qquad$ (4.8)
(ii) $f(c_i)$ and $f(b_i)$ have opposite signs. $\qquad$ (4.9)

If (4.8) holds, then (4.7) has a solution between a_i and c_i, and we define

$$a_{i+1} = a_i, \quad b_{i+1} = c_i$$

If instead (4.9) holds, then (4.7) has a solution between c_i and b_i and we define

$$a_{i+1} = c_i, \quad b_{i+1} = b_i$$

In either case the new interval $[a_{i+1}, b_{i+1}]$ contains a solution and its length $h_{i+1} = b_{i+1} - a_{i+1}$ is half the length h_i of the previous interval $[a_i, b_i]$. The formal algorithm is summarised below.

Algorithm 4.1 Bisection method

(i) Find an interval $[a_0, b_0]$ such that $f(a_0)f(b_0) \leqslant 0$. For $i = 0, 1, 2, \ldots$:
(ii) Calculate $f(c_i)$ where $c_i = \tfrac{1}{2}(a_i + b_i)$. Define $a_{i+1} = a_i$, $b_{i+1} = c_i$ if $f(a_i)f(c_i) \leqslant 0$. Define $a_{i+1} = c_i, b_{i+1} = b_i$ otherwise.
(iii) Repeat until $h_{i+1} = b_{i+1} - a_{i+1}$ is smaller than a specified accuracy ε, and then set $s = c_{i+1}$.

Example

For the function (4.7), if we retain just three decimal places throughout the arithmetic, the values obtained for a_i, b_i and their corresponding signs are given in Table 4.2.

From the results we deduce that the solution s of (4.7) satisfies

$$0.567 < s < 0.568$$

Table 4.2 Bisection for $f(x) = e^{-x} - x = 0$

i	a_i	c_i	b_i	h_i	sign (a_i)	sign (c_i)	sign (b_i)
0	.5	.625	.75	.25	+	−	−
1	.5	.562	.625	.125	+	+	−
2	.562	.593	.625	.063	+	−	−
3	.562	.578	.593	.031	+	−	−
4	.562	.570	.578	.016	+	−	−
5	.562	.566	.570	.008	+	+	−
6	.566	.568	.570	.004	+	−	−
7	.566	.567	.568	.002	+	+	−
8	.567	.5675	.568	.001			

and we choose the approximation

$$s \simeq 0.5675$$

which has an error of at most 0.0005. No further accuracy can be achieved in three decimal arithmetic.

It is clear that the bisection method converges for any equation (4.1) in which $f(x)$ is continuous. Moreover it always converges at the same rate, since the bisection process is essentially independent of the nature of the function $f(x)$. Indeed the (truncation) error e_i, say, after bisection i is at most h_{i+1}, the length of the interval $[a_{i+1}, b_{i+1}]$, and so the error e_{i+1} after the next bisection is at most h_{i+2} which is precisely half as large. Applying this rule repetitively from the initial interval, we deduce that

$$|e_i| \leqslant h_{i+1} = 2^{-(i+1)}h_0 \tag{4.10}$$

The inequality (4.10) tells us, *before* performing any calculations, a bound on the error that will be obtained after i bisections. Such a valuable type of bound is termed, from the Latin, an *a priori* error bound.

Taking logs to base 10 in (4.10) and setting $\varepsilon = |e_i|$, it follows that

$$(i + 1) \leqslant \log_{10}(h_0/\varepsilon)/\log_{10} 2$$

i.e.

$$i \leqslant [(\log_{10}(h_0) - \log_{10}(\varepsilon))/\log_{10}(2)] - 1 \tag{4.11}$$

We have thus obtained in (4.11) an *a priori* bound on the number of iterations required to achieve an accuracy ε, starting from an interval of length h_0. We therefore know *beforehand* how many bisections will be required. For example, if an accuracy of .001 is to be achieved, then $\varepsilon = 0.0005$ and $h_0 = 0.25$, and hence

$$i \leq [\log_{10} 500/\log_{10} 2] - 1 = 7.966 \qquad (4.12)$$

Since fractions of iterations are meaningless, we deduce that at most 8 iterations are required. In Table 4.2 we observe that this is precisely the number that were required in practice.

The BASIC program for the bisection method is given below. It is tested on the problem (4.4), namely

$$f(x) = \tan x - 2x = 0$$

which has a non-zero solution between $\pi/4$ and $\pi/2$ (Figure 2.2). A solution is sought successfully in the range $[.8, 1.4]$ and unsuccessfully in the range $[.4, .8]$.

Program 4.1 BISECT: Bisection method

```
LIST
BISECT

10   REM- BISECT: CALCULATES A ROOT OF F(X)=0 BY BISECTION METHOD
20   REM- USER SPECIFIES AN INTERVAL [A,B] CONTAINING THE ROOT
30   PRINT "INTERVAL END POINTS A,B ";
40   INPUT A,B
50   PRINT "ABSOLUTE ACCURACY REQUIRED ";
60   INPUT E
70   I=0
80   H=B-A
90   P=FNF(A)*FNF(B)
100  IF 0>=P THEN 130
110  PRINT "X DOES NOT LIE BETWEEN INITIAL A AND B"
120  GO TO 320
130  PRINT "ITERATION:","A:","B:"
140  I=I+1
150  H=.5*H
160  C=A+H
170  P=FNF(A)*FNF(C)
180  IF P>0 THEN 210
190  B=C
200  GO TO 220
210  A=C
220  PRINT I,A,B
230  E1=.5*H
240  IF E1>E THEN 140
250  PRINT "ABSOLUTE ACCURACY ACHIEVED"
260  PRINT "X LIES BETWEEN";A;"AND";B
270  X=.5*(A+B)
280  PRINT "APPROXIMATION TO X :";X
290  PRINT "MAX ERROR :";E1
300  REM-SPECIFY FUNCTION F(X)
310  DEF FNF(X)=TAN(X)-2*X
320  END

Ready


RUN
BISECT

INTERVAL END POINTS A,B ? .8,1.4
ABSOLUTE ACCURACY REQUIRED ? .0001
ITERATION:        A:              B:
1                 1.1             1.4
2                 1.1             1.25
3                 1.1             1.175
4                 1.1375          1.175
5                 1.15625         1.175
6                 1.15625         1.16562
7                 1.16094         1.16562
```

```
8              1.16328        1.16562
9              1.16445        1.16562
10             1.16504        1.16562
11             1.16533        1.16562
12             1.16548        1.16562
ABSOLUTE ACCURACY ACHIEVED
X LIES BETWEEN 1.16548 AND 1.16562
APPROXIMATION TO X : 1.16555
MAX ERROR : .732422E-04
Ready
```

```
RUN
BISECT

INTERVAL END POINTS A,B ? .4,.8
ABSOLUTE ACCURACY REQUIRED ? .0001
X DOES NOT LIE BETWEEN INITIAL A AND B
Ready
```

Program notes

(1) $f(x)$ is specified in instruction 310 by a defined function FNF(X). Any new $f(x)$ may be specified by a new instruction 310.

4.4 Fixed-point iteration

In the bisection method we were really concerned with intervals containing a solution rather than with *points* which approximate the solution. The methods in the remainder of this chapter are, however, concerned with points rather than intervals. The basic approach is to guess a solution and then, by using the form of the equation, to obtain successively better approximations. These approximations are obtained by performing certain simple calculations over and over again, and such an approach is called 'iteration'.

For the first and most basic iteration method to be discussed, the fixed-point iteration, the procedure is as follows. Take the given equation

$$f(x) = 0 \qquad (4.13)$$

and rewrite it in the form

$$x = g(x) \qquad (4.14)$$

for some choice of a function $g(x)$. Note, however, that this choice is not unique. For example the quadratic equation

$$f(x) = x^2 - 4x + 1 = 0 \qquad (4.15)$$

can be rewritten in (infinitely) many such ways, including such obvious choices as

$$x = 4 - 1/x, \quad x = (1 + x^2)/4, \quad x = \sqrt{(4x - 1)}. \qquad (4.16)$$

The chosen function $g(x)$ on the right hand side is called the 'iteration function' and is used to determine a succession of values x_1, $x_2, \ldots$ of x, starting from an initial guess x_0 for the solution. We already know (from Section 4.2) an interval of values containing the solution, say the interval $[a, b]$ (i.e. all points x such that $a \leqslant x \leqslant b$), and so we make an initial choice of x_0 somewhere in $[a, b]$.

Consider in particular the third iteration function in (4.16), that is

$$g(x) = \sqrt{(4x - 1)}$$

and suppose that we know that (4.15) has a solution in $[3, 4]$. (The latter is obvious, since $f(3) = -2 < 0$ and $f(4) = 1 > 0$). Choose $x_0 = 4$ as the guess for the solution, and define new values x_1, $x_2, \ldots$ as follows:

$$x_1 = g(x_0) = \sqrt{[4(4) - 1]} \qquad = 3.8730$$
$$x_2 = g(x_1) = \sqrt{[4(3.8730) - 1]} = 3.8068$$
$$x_3 = g(x_2) = \sqrt{[4(3.8068) - 1]} = 3.7719$$

etc. Clearly this simple procedure is converging successfully to the larger 3.7321 of the two roots $2 \pm \sqrt{3}$ of Equation (4.15). For clarity we now give a formal statement of this algorithm, based on a single repeated assignment, and follow this with a precise list of criteria which are sufficient to guarantee its convergence.

Algorithm 4.2 Fixed-point iteration for $x = g(x)$

  (i) Choose an initial estimate of the solution x_0.
 (ii) For $i = 1, 2, 3, \ldots$ define $x_i = g(x_{i-1})$.

Then, provided Criteria 4.2 hold, the values of x_i approach the solution s of (4.13).

Criteria 4.2 Convergence of $x_i = g(x_{i-1})$ on $[a, b]$

  (i) There is exactly one solution s of (4.13) (or (4.14)) in $[a, b]$.
 (ii) x_0 is in $[a, b]$.
(iii) For any x in $[a, b]$, the value $g(x)$ lies in $[a, b]$.
 (iv) $|g'(x)| < 1$ for *all* x in $[a, b]$.

In some instances it may be difficult or even impossible to check the Criteria 4.2. In that case the algorithm can still be tried out, but there will be no knowing in advance whether or not it will converge.

4.4.1 *Example*

To illustrate the use of Algorithm 4.2 and Criteria 4.2, consider again the quadratic equation

$$f(x) = x^2 - 4x + 1 = 0 \quad \text{for} \quad x \text{ in } [3, 4] \qquad (4.17)$$

(We are not, however, suggesting that the Algorithm should ever be used to solve a quadratic.) In Table 4.3 the iterates $x_0, x_1, \ldots$ are given for the two choices of iteration functions, (a) $g(x) = 4 - 1/x$ and (b) $g(x) = (1 + x^2)/4$, starting in each case from an initial guess of $x_0 = 4$. Clearly the Algorithm is converging for choice (a) and diverging for choice (b). The key condition in Criteria 4.2 is condition (iv), namely $|g'(x)| < 1$. For choice (a) $g'(x) = 1/x^2$ and so $|g'(x)| \leqslant 1/9$ throughout $[3, 4]$. For choice (b), $g'(x) = x/2$ and so $|g'(x)| \geqslant 3/2$ throughout $[3, 4]$. Clearly choice (b) breaks the criteria.

Consider the remaining conditions (i), (ii), (iii), of Criteria 4.2 for choice (a).

Condition (i): Clearly (4.17) has a unique solution $2 + \sqrt{3}$ in $[3, 4]$. However, an algebraic argument can be given in the pattern of Section 4.2 as follows. From (4.17),

$$f(3) = -2, \qquad f(4) = +1$$
$$f'(x) = 2(x - 2) > 0 \quad \text{throughout } [3, 4]$$

Thus f increases steadily (since its gradient is of one sign) from -2 at $x = 3$ to $+1$ at $x = 4$, and hence it must have precisely one zero in $[3, 4]$. As an alternative approach, a simple sketch might be used to confirm that f has just one change of sign.

Condition (ii): x_0 has been chosen in $[3, 4]$ as required

Condition (iii): $g(x) = 4 - 1/x$. This function increases as x increases in $[3, 4]$.

Table 4.3 Iterates for $x^2 - 4x + 1 = 0$

i	(a) $g(x) = 4 - 1/x$ $x_i = g(x_{i-1})$	(b) $g(x) = (1 + x^2)/4$ $x_i = g(x_{i-1})$
0	4	4
1	3.75	4.25
2	3.733333	4.765625
3	3.7321	5.927795
4	3.73206	9.034690

Thus

$$4 - 1/3 \leqslant g(x) \leqslant 4 - 1/4 \qquad \text{for any } x \text{ in } [3, 4]$$

and hence

$$3 \leqslant g(x) \leqslant 4.$$

So $g(x)$ is in $[3, 4]$ for all x in $[3, 4]$ as required.

4.4.2 *BASIC program*

A BASIC program for the fixed-point iteration is given below. For safety we have inserted two escape clauses. Firstly, we have put a specified limit on the number of iterations to be performed, in case the iteration does not converge to s. Secondly, to save computer time we have stopped the iteration as soon as i reaches a value for which

$$\left| \frac{x_i - x_{i-1}}{x_i} \right| < \varepsilon$$

that is to say that x_{i-1} and x_i agree to a specified relative accuracy of ε. (The character ε is represented by the letter E in the program.) Please note that this does not imply that x_i has converged to this relative accuracy; it is merely a rough yardstick for gauging the accuracy of x_i. For example, if convergence is slow, it is quite possible for x_{i-1} and x_i to agree to 4 figures but only be correct to 3 figures.

Program 4.2 FIXITE: Fixed point iteration

```
LIST
FIXITE

10 REM- FIXITE:  1) SOLVES X=G(X) BY FIXED-PT ITERATION
20 REM-             IF G' < 1 IN MAGNITUDE NEAR SOLUTION
30 REM-          2) TO APPLY NEWTON'S METHOD TO F(X)=0
40 REM-             SET G(X)=X-F(X)/F'(X).
50 DIM X(30)
60 PRINT "INITIAL ESTIMATE X(0) ";
70 INPUT X(0)
80 PRINT "MAXIMUM NUMBER OF ITERATIONS ";
90 INPUT M
100 PRINT "REQUIRED RELATIVE ACCURACY ";
110 INPUT E
120 I=1
130 REM- ITERATION DETERMINES X(I) FROM X(I-1)
140 X(I)=FNG(X(I-1))
150 E1=ABS(1-X(I-1)/X(I))
160 IF E1>E GO TO 190
170 PRINT "RELATIVE ACCURACY ATTAINED"
180 GO TO 250
190 IF M>I GO TO 230
200 PRINT "MAXIMUM NUMBER OF ITERATIONS REACHED"
210 GO TO 250
```

```
220 REM-   UPDATE I
230 I=I+1
240 GO TO 140
250 PRINT "ITERATED X VALUES:"
260 FOR L=0 TO I
270 PRINT X(L),
280 NEXT L
290 REM- DEFINITION OF FUNCTION G(X)
300 DEF FNG(X)=SQR(4*X-1)
310 END

Ready



RUN
FIXITE

INITIAL ESTIMATE X(0) ? 4
MAXIMUM NUMBER OF ITERATIONS ? 10
REQUIRED RELATIVE ACCURACY ? .001
RELATIVE ACCURACY ATTAINED
ITERATED X VALUES:
 4              3.87298       3.80683       3.77191       3.75335       3.74345
      3.73815       3.73532
Ready



300 DEF FNG(X)=(2*X^3+1)/(3*X^2-1)
RUN
FIXITE

INITIAL ESTIMATE X(0) ? 1.3
MAXIMUM NUMBER OF ITERATIONS ? 10
REQUIRED RELATIVE ACCURACY ? .00001
RELATIVE ACCURACY ATTAINED
ITERATED X VALUES:
 1.3            1.32531       1.32472       1.32472
Ready
```

Program notes

(1) In Sample Run 1, the third iteration function of (4.16) is applied to solve (4.15).
(2) This program may also be used to implement Newton's method, as described in Section 4.5 below. Sample Run 2 relates to such an application.

4.4.3 *Convergence*

The pattern of Algorithm 4.2 and Program 4.2 is illustrated in Figures 4.2(a), 4.2(b). The solution s of (4.14) is the ordinate at the intersection of the line $y = x$ and the curve $y = g(x)$. Starting at the ordinate $x = x_0$, the algorithm moves parallel to $0y$ to meet $y = g(x)$ at P_0 and then parallel to $0x$ to meet $y = x$ at Q_0. The ordinate Q_0 is the new approximation $x_1 = g(x_0)$ to s, and the algorithm continues in the same way to obtain further approximations $x_2, x_3, \ldots$. It is clear that in Figure 4.2(a), where the gradient of $g(x)$ is never greater than one in magnitude, the values x_0, $x_1, x_2, \ldots$ are converging to the solution s. However, in Figure

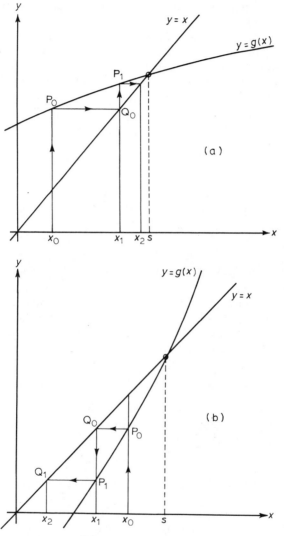

Figure 4.2 Fixed-point iteration (*a*) $|g'(x)|<1$ (*b*) $|g'(x)|>1$

4.2(b) where $g(x)$ has a gradient greater than one the algorithm can be seen to be diverging.

Thus the necessity for condition (iv) of Criteria 4.2 has been verified in Figures 4.2(a) and 4.2(b). The necessity for the remaining conditions is also apparent. Condition (i) ensures that $y = x$ and $y = g(x)$ cross just once, and conditions (ii) and (iii) ensure that $x_0, x_1, x_2, \ldots$ all lie in a fixed interval $[a, b]$ (so that if we start in an interval in which $|g'(x)| < 1$ we never leave that interval).

The key condition (iv) that $|g'(x)| < 1$ can also be justified mathematically. The Mean Value Theorem establishes that

$$g(x_1) - g(x_0) = (x_1 - x_0)g'(x^*)$$

for some x^* between x_0 and x_1. Since $g(x_0) = x_1$ and $g(x_1) = x_2$, it follows that

$$x_2 - x_1 = (x_1 - x_0)g'(x^*) \qquad (4.18)$$

and hence if $|g'(x)| < 1$ then

$$|x_2 - x_1| = |x_1 - x_0| \, |g'(x^*)| < |x_1 - x_0|$$

Similarly

$$|x_3 - x_2| < |x_2 - x_1|,$$

etc. Thus the distance between consecutive pairs of iterates is decreasing, and (by refining the analysis further) it is easy to show that this distance approaches zero and so the algorithm converges.

We note that (subject to Criteria 4.2) the algorithm converges for *any* starting value x_0 in the interval $[a, b]$, and for this reason the algorithm is said to be *globally covergent*.

4.4.4 *Rate of convergence*

Although Criteria 4.2 guarantee convergence, it is not clear how rapid this convergence is. If x_i is an iterate and s is the solution, then by definition

$$x_i = g(x_{i-1}) \quad \text{and} \quad s = g(s)$$

Hence the (truncation) error e_i in the iterate x_i is given by

$$e_i = x_i - s = g(x_{i-1}) - g(s) \qquad (4.19)$$

By a Taylor series expansion,

$$g(x_{i-1}) = g(s) + (x_{i-1} - s)g'(s) + \tfrac{1}{2}(x_{i-1} - s)^2 g''(s) + \cdots$$

and hence from (4.19)

$$e_i = e_{i-1}g'(s) + \tfrac{1}{2}(e_{i-1})^2 g''(s) + \cdots \qquad (4.20)$$

Let us assume that the constant $g'(s)$ is not zero (see Newton's method below for this special case). Then, since e_i and e_{i-1} are small, for i sufficiently large

$$|e_i| \simeq C |e_{i-1}| \qquad (4.21)$$

where

$$C = |g'(s)| \quad \text{and} \quad C < 1$$

by Criteria 4.2.

Equation (4.21) tells us that (by Criteria 4.2) for every i the error at step i is a constant (less than unity) times the error at step $i - 1$, and so the error is being reduced at a constant rate. Such convergence is termed *linear convergence*. We shall call the constant C the 'linear convergence constant'. In practical terms it is easy to verify that we obtain $\log_{10}(1/C)$ correct decimal places of the solution for every iteration (e.g. for $C = .01$ we obtain 2 correct decimals per iteration). Note that convergence is slow unless C is rather smaller than 1, and indeed in general the agreement of two consecutive answers to a certain number of figures is not a guarantee that the answers are accurate to that number of figures.

Table 4.4 Linear convergence for $g(x) = 4 - 1/x$

i	x_i	$e_i = x_i - s$	$|e_i|/|e_{i-1}|$
0	4	0.2679	
1	3.75	0.01795	.06700
2	3.73333333	0.001283	.07148
3	3.73214286	0.00009205	.07175
4	3.732057416	0.000006608	.07179
5	3.732051282	0.000000474	.0717

Linear convergence is illustrated in Table 4.4 for the iteration function

$$g(x) = 4 - 1/x$$

In addition to the iterated values x_i, the errors $e_i = x_i - s$ and ratios of errors $|e_i|/|e_{i-1}|$ have been calculated. Here $g'(x) = x^{-2}$ and so

$$C = |g'(s)| = s^{-2} = (3.73205)^{-2} = .071797$$

and clearly the error ratio $|e_i|/|e_{i-1}|$ is converging to this value as predicted. The number of correct decimal places of s that are obtained per iteration (for i large) is

$$\log_{10}(1/C) = \log_{10}(3.732^2) = 1.14$$

and it is clear that a little more than one decimal per iteration is indeed being achieved in Table 4.4.

Note that the results in Table 4.4 have been calculated to a higher accuracy than is normally possible in BASIC, in order to illustrate clearly the nature of the convergence.

4.4.5 *An a posteriori error bound*

For the bisection method, it was possible to give an upper bound (4.10) on the size of the truncation error at any stage in the method. This was an *a priori* bound which predicted the accuracy attainable *before* the algorithm was used. For the fixed-point iteration, we now give an *a posteriori* bound for the truncation error, which is determined *after* the iteration has been applied.

Suppose an iteration function $g(x)$ is chosen so that Criteria 4.2 are satisfied for some interval $[a, b]$ of x, and suppose that condition (iv) of the Criteria is replaced by the more specific condition:

$$|g'(x)| \leq L < 1 \qquad \text{in } [a, b] \qquad (4.22)$$

where L is some (not unique) constant which is determined. Then it can be shown that the (truncation) error $e_i = x_i - s$ at iteration i satisfies

$$|e_i| \leq (1 - L)^{-1} |x_i - x_{i+1}| \qquad (4.23)$$

Thus the error in x_i can be bounded rigorously, once x_i and the next iterate x_{i+1} are known.

For example for the quadratic equation (4.17) and the iteration function $g(x) = 4 - 1/x$, (see Table 4.4) it follows that

$$|g'(x)| \leq 1/9 < 1 \qquad \text{in } [3, 4]$$

and so (4.22) holds for $L = 1/9$. Hence from (4.23) we obtain the bound:

$$|e_i| \leq 1.125 |x_i - x_{i+1}|$$

For the value x_4 calculated in Table 4.4, we use the value of x_5 to obtain the bound:

$$|e_4| = |x_4 - s| \leq 1.125 |3.7320574 - 3.7320513| = 0.0000069$$

Since the actual error is 0.0000066, the bound is very realistic in this case.

The derivation of (4.23) is briefly as follows. From Criteria 4.2 and inequality (4.22), it is easy (compare (4.18)) to deduce that

$$x_{i+1} - x_i = (x_i - x_{i-1})g'(x^*) \qquad \text{for some } x^* \text{ in } [a, b]$$

and hence

$$|x_{i+1} - x_i| \leqslant L\,|x_i - x_{i-1}|\qquad (L < 1)\text{ for all }i.$$

Then

$$|x_i - s| = |x_i - x_\infty| \leqslant |x_i - x_{i+1}| + |x_{i+1} - x_{i+2}| + |x_{i+2} - x_{i+3}| +$$
$$+ \cdots \leqslant |x_i - x_{i+1}|\,(1 + L + L^2 + \cdots) = (1 - L)^{-1}\,|x_i - x_{i+1}|.$$

4.5 Newton's method

The linear convergence of the fixed-point iteration can be rather slow unless $C = |f'(s)|$ is fairly small. For example for $C = .5$ the error is halved at each iteration, and we need three or four iterations to obtain each correct decimal place of the solution. Often, therefore, a linearly convergent algorithm is only used to obtain a crude approximation to the solution, and a second algorithm offering faster convergence (but typically less reliability) is used to obtain an accurate solution. A good example of such a second algorithm is Newton's method, which we shall introduce as a special case of Algorithm 4.2.

The equation

$$f(x) = 0 \tag{4.24}$$

can always be rewritten in the form

$$x = g(x) \tag{4.25}$$

for the special choice of iteration function

$$g(x) \equiv x - f(x)/f'(x) \tag{4.26}$$

Clearly equations (4.24) and (4.25) are equivalent for this choice of $g(x)$. The corresponding iteration

$$x_i = g(x_{i-1}) = x_{i-1} - f(x_{i-1})/f'(x_{i-1}) \tag{4.27}$$

is called *Newton's method*.

In Figure 4.3 the progress of Newton's method is illustrated. The solution s is the intersection of the curve $y = f(x)$ with $0x$. At the ordinate x_0, a tangent is drawn through P_0 on $y = f(x)$ to meet the x axis at an angle θ at the point x_1. Clearly

$$f(x_0) = (x_0 - x_1)\tan\theta$$

$$\tan\theta = \left(\frac{dy}{dx}\right)_{x_0} = f'(x_0)$$

and so

$$x_1 = x_0 - f(x_0)/f'(x_0)$$

Thus x_1 is indeed the next iterate in Newton's method, and it is clear from Figure 4.3 that the sequence of iterates will approach s very rapidly.

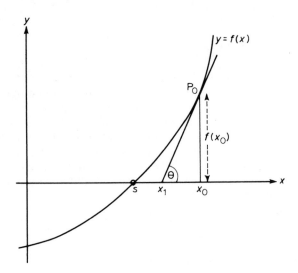

Figure 4.3 Newton's method

Now from (4.26)

$$g'(x) = 1 - \frac{[f'(x)]^2 - f(x)f''(x)}{[f'(x)]^2} = \frac{f(x)f''(x)}{[f'(x)]^2} \qquad (4.28)$$

and, since $f(x) = 0$ at the solution $x = s$, it follows that

$$g'(s) = 0$$

(This was the exceptional case excluded from the discussion of Section 4.4). Substituting this value in the expression (4.20) for the error e_i,

$$e_i = \tfrac{1}{2}(e_{i-1})^2 g''(s) + \tfrac{1}{6}(e_{i-1})^3 g'''(s) + \cdots$$

and hence for large i

$$|e_i| \simeq D\,|e_{i-1}|^2$$

where
$$D = \tfrac{1}{2} |g''(s)|$$

Thus the error at step i is proportional to the *square* of the error at step $i - 1$ and, since these are small quantities, the error is reduced greatly at each iteration. This type of convergence is termed *quadratic convergence*. In practical terms it means that the number of correct decimal places is approximately doubled at each iteration. Indeed if two consecutive results agree to a certain number of figures, then they are not only both correct to that number of figures but the second result is correct to nearly twice that number.

It is not necessary to write a new BASIC program in order to implement Newton's method. We may simply use Program 4.2 with FNG defined as the appropriate function (4.26). For example, to solve

$$f(x) = x^3 - x - 1 = 0 \qquad (4.29)$$

by Newton's method, we take

$$g(x) = x - \frac{x^3 - x - 1}{3x^2 - 1} = \frac{2x^3 + 1}{3x^2 - 1}$$

and define FNG by the statement

300 DEF FNG(X) = (2*X ^ 3 + 1)/(3*X ^ 2 - 1)

This is illustrated in Sample Run 2 of Program 4.2.

To illustrate Newton's method in more detail and demonstrate its convergence properties, rather accurate results are given in Table 4.5 for Equation (4.29), starting from $x_0 = 1.3$. Convergence is seen to be extremely rapid, and the number of correct decimal figures can be estimated easily. Since x_0 and x_1 agree to two figures, and x_1 and x_2 agree to four figures, we deduce that x_0, x_1, x_2 are respectively correct to about two, four, and eight figures (since numbers of correct figures are approximately doubled at each step). Note also that, as predicted, $|e_i|/|e_{i-1}|^2$ is approximately a constant value D ($\simeq 0.932$ here).

Table 4.5 Newton's method for $x^3 - x - 1 = 0$

i	x_i	$e_i = x_i - s$	No. of correct figures	$|e_i|/|e_{i-1}|^2$
0	1.3000000	−.0247	2	—
1	1.325307125	.000589	4	0.965
2	1.324718281	.000000324	7	0.934
	($s = 1.324717957$)			

4.5.1 *Convergence of Newton's method*

Since $g'(x) = 0$ in Newton's method at the solution $x = s$, it is clear that there must be some small interval $[a, b]$ around the root s throughout which $|g'(x)| < 1$. Hence Condition (iv) is satisfied in Criteria 4.2, and it is not difficult to show similarly that Conditions (ii) and (iii) are also satisfied in a small interval. So Newton's method will *always* converge if the initial value x_0 is chosen *sufficiently close* to s. Such convergence is termed *local convergence*. (By way of comparison Algorithm 4.2 either converges globally on an interval $[a, b]$ or not at all; in particular if $|f'(s)| > 1$ the algorithm does not converge however close x_0 is chosen to s.)

4.5.2 *Combined algorithms*

A more versatile algorithm can be obtained by combining the complementary features of Algorithm 4.2 (for a simple choice of $g(x)$) and Newton's method. The fixed-point algorithm has global linear convergence (subject to Criteria 4.2) and is therefore reliable but slow, while Newton's method has local quadratic convergence and is therefore less reliable but fast. Indeed Program 4.2 can easily be adapted to shift from the first chosen iteration function to the Newton iteration function (4.26) as soon as the solution has been obtained to say two or three significant figures. Such an algorithm is left as an exercise to the reader.

Alternatively we might use the bisection method (Algorithm 4.1) to locate a root to a limited accuracy, and then shift to Newton's method to obtain high accuracy. (See Problem 7 below.)

4.6 The secant method

There are disadvantages in the methods of Section 4.4 and Section 4.5. For a fixed-point iteration (Algorithm 4.2) some skill or luck is required in choosing an iteration function for which $|g'(x)| < 1$, and even so the iteration is only linearly convergent. For Newton's method it is necessary to calculate the gradient $f'(x)$ of $f(x)$, and this can be very expensive. In this section we introduce the secant method, which is very similar to Newton's method but does not involve a gradient. There are two small prices to pay. Firstly, the method calculates an iterate x_i from two previous iterates x_{i-1} and x_{i-2} rather than one, and so it requires two starting values x_0 and x_1. Secondly, the ultimate convergence achieved is not quite as fast as that of Newton's method.

The secant method is based on Newton's method. However,

instead of drawing a tangent through the point P_0 with ordinate x_0 (see Figure 4.4) a secant is drawn through the pair of points P_0 and P_1 with ordinates x_0 and x_1. It is clear from Figure 4.4 that, once the iterates are close to the solution, the secant method has an effect closely resembling that of Newton's method, since the secant has a direction close to that of the tangent. The algorithm differs

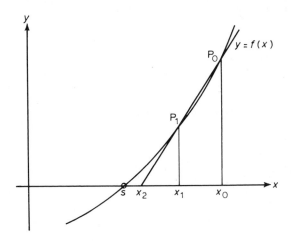

Figure 4.4 Secant method

from Newton's method (4.27) only in the replacement of $f'(x_{i-1})$ by $[f(x_{i-1}) - f(x_{i-2})]/(x_{i-1} - x_{i-2})$. The algorithm and BASIC program are as follows.

Algorithm 4.3 The secant method

(i) Choose two initial estimates x_0 and x_1 for the solution s.
(ii) For $i = 2, 3, 4, \ldots$ define x_i from

$$x_i = x_{i-1} - f(x_{i-1}) \frac{(x_{i-1} - x_{i-2})}{f(x_{i-1}) - f(x_{i-2})} \tag{4.30}$$

Program 4.3 SECANT: Secant method

```
LIST
SECANT

10 REM- SECANT: SOLVES F(X)=0 BY SECANT METHOD
20 REM- X(0),X(1) MUST BE SUFFICIENTLY CLOSE TO SOLUTION
30 DIM X(30)
40 PRINT "STARTING VALUES X(0),X(1)";
50 INPUT X(0),X(1)
60 PRINT "MAXIMUM NUMBER OF ITERATIONS";
```

```
70 INPUT M
80 PRINT "RELATIVE ACCURACY REQUIRED";
90 INPUT E
100 I=2
110 REM- ITERATION FOR X(I)
120 A=FNF(X(I-1))
130 B=FNF(X(I-2))
140 E1=-A*(X(I-1)-X(I-2))/(A-B)
150 X(I)=X(I-1)+E1
160 IF ABS(E1/X(I))>E GO TO 190
170 PRINT "RELATIVE ACCURACY ATTAINED"
180 GO TO 250
190 IF M>I GO TO 220
200 PRINT "MAXIMUM NUMBER OF ITERATIONS REACHED"
210 GO TO 250
220 REM- UPDATE X VALUES
230 I=I+1
240 GO TO 120
250 PRINT "ITERATED X VALUES :"
260 FOR L=1 TO I
270 PRINT X(L),
280 NEXT L
290 REM-DEFINITION OF FUNCTION F(X)
300 DEF FNF(X)=X^3-X-1
310 END

Ready


RUN
SECANT

STARTING VALUES X(0),X(1)? 1,1.5
MAXIMUM NUMBER OF ITERATIONS? 10
RELATIVE ACCURACY REQUIRED? .00001
RELATIVE ACCURACY ATTAINED
ITERATED X VALUES :
 1.5          1.26667      1.31596      1.32521      1.32471      1.32472

Ready
```

Program notes

(1) Safety clauses are again included to stop the program after a specified number of iterations or at a specified relative accuracy.
(2) Instruction 300 at the end of the program uses the defined function FNF(X) to specify $f(x)$, and so in its present form the program is designed to solve the equation

$$f(x) = x^3 - x - 1 = 0$$

Any other equation can be solved, simply by appropriately redefining FNF(X). Alternatively, a function subroutine, ending with the instruction FNEND, may be used to define FNF(X).

Like Newton's method, this algorithm is *locally convergent*. However, it is not quadratically convergent, and in fact it can be proved that for large i

$$|e_i| \simeq c \,|e_{i-1}|^p \qquad (4.31)$$

where $p \simeq 1.62$ (see Problem 11 below).
A sequence of values $x_0, x_1, \ldots, x_{i-1}, x_i, \ldots$ for which (4.31)

holds for some specified p is said to have *order of convergence p*. So the secant method has order of convergence 1.62, compared with the order of convergence 2 of Newton's method. Clearly the number of correct decimal places at iteration i is approximately $p = 1.62$ times the number correct at $i - 1$, and so the convergence is only marginally inferior to that of Newton's method. Methods, such as the secant and Newton's which have an order of convergence greater than one are sometimes described as having *superlinear convergence* to emphasise their superiority over linearly convergent methods.

Since the secant method is fast, we must expect it to be unreliable, and this is demonstrated in Figure 4.5, where the method fails on a 'wiggly' but continuous function.

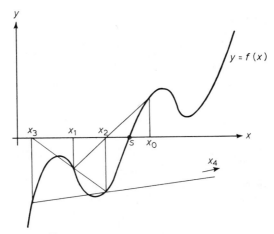

Figure 4.5 Secant – unreliable

4.7 Polynomial equations

Quadratic equations (Section 3.8) and cubic and quartic equations such as (4.2) and (4.3) are all examples of 'polynomial equations'. These take the general form

$$p_n(x) = a_0 x^n + a_1 x^{n-1} + a_2 x^{n-2} + \cdots + a_n = 0 \quad (4.32)$$

where n is the degree of the equation, $a_0, a_1, \ldots, a_n$ are given real 'coefficients' and x is the required solution. The form (4.32) is a rather special example of a nonlinear algebraic equation, and so, rather than use a method such as fixed-point iteration, it is worthwhile to seek a new method specially designed for the problem.

The 'fundamental theorem of algebra' tells us that (4.32) has precisely n solutions $s_1, \ldots, s_n$ for x, provided that we allow x to be complex and count multiple solutions appropriately. For example, $x^2 - 2x + 1 = 0$ has two solutions $x = 1, 1$, and $x^3 - 1 = 0$ has three solutions $x = 1, \frac{1}{2}(-1 \pm i\sqrt{3})$. However, another basic theorem tells us that it is in general impossible to obtain exact formulae for solutions of (4.32). The quadratic equation of Section 3.8 was a very special and simple example, and a completely different approach is required for the general equation (4.32). Many methods have been devised, and almost all are based on iteration.

4.7.1 *Bernoulli's method*

A neat algorithm may be obtained by relating equation (4.32) to the linear recurrence relation

$$a_0 x_i + a_1 x_{i-1} + a_2 x_{i-2} + \cdots + a_n x_{i-n} = 0$$

If n 'initial values' $x_0, x_1, \ldots, x_{n-1}$ are specified, then a sequence of values $x_n, x_{n+1}, x_{n+2}, \ldots$ may be explicitly calculated from this relation by simply writing

$$x_i = -(a_1 x_{i-1} + a_2 x_{i-2} + \cdots + a_n x_{i-n})/a_0 \qquad (4.33)$$

for $i = n, n + 1, n + 2, \ldots$.

Note that this is just a generalisation of the three-term recurrence relation discussed in Section 3.9 and solved in Program 3.9. The reader is therefore advised to read that section again, as a simple introduction to the present discussion.

Now it can be shown that we can express x_i in the form

$$x_i = c_1(s_1)^i + c_2(s_2)^i + \cdots + c_n(s_n)^i \qquad (4.34)$$

where $c_1, c_2, \ldots, c_n$ are some (unknown) constants and $s_1, s_2, \ldots, s_n$ are the n solutions of (4.32). Having determined a sequence of values $x_0, x_1, \ldots, x_n, x_{n+1}, x_{n+2}, \ldots$, it is now possible to use (4.34) to determine a solution of (4.32). We shall describe an algorithm for the case in which the largest solution in magnitude of (4.32) is *real*.

Suppose that s_1 is the largest root in magnitude, so that

$$|s_1| > |s_j| \qquad \text{for } j = 2, 3, \ldots, n.$$

Then *for large i*, from (4.34),

$$x_i \simeq c_1(s_1)^i$$

since $(s_1)^i$ dominates $(s_2)^i, (s_3)^i, \ldots$ for i sufficiently large. So the ratio of two consecutive x's, namely the quantity

$$u_i = x_i/x_{i-1}$$

has the property that, for large i,

$$u_i \simeq \frac{c_1(s_1)^i}{c_1(s_1)^{i-1}} = s_1$$

More precisely

$$\lim_{i \to \infty} u_i = s_1$$

So the largest root s_1 may simply be found by taking ratios $u_1, u_2,$ $u_3, \ldots, u_i, \ldots$ of consecutive x's and observing the value approached by u_i as i becomes large. This is *Bernoulli's method*.

Example   Consider applying Bernoulli's method to the quadratic equation

$$x^2 - x - 2 = 0$$

This equation has roots $s_1, s_2 = 2, -1$, and so the method should give values for u_i which approach 2 for large i. The associated linear recurrence relation (compare (4.33)) is

$$x_i - x_{i-1} - 2x_{i-2} = 0$$

which is precisely the recurrence relation obtained for the three colour problem in Section 3.9 above. Then, for some choice of x_0 and x_1, we may calculate $x_2, x_3, \ldots$ from the formula (compare (4.33))

$$x_i = x_{i-1} + 2x_{i-2} \qquad (i = 2, 3, 4, \ldots)$$

and hence determine ratios

$$u_i = x_i/x_{i-1}. \qquad (i = 2, 3, 4, \ldots)$$

If we choose

$$x_0 = 3, \quad x_1 = 0$$

then we obtain the values in the first two columns of Table 4.6, which correspond precisely to the solution of the three colour problem of Section 3.9. As expected the values of u_i are correctly approaching the dominant root ($s_1 = 2$), and from the value of u_i for $i = 12$ we may deduce that

$$s_1 \simeq 2.003$$

The theory is simple to follow in this example. The expression

Table 4.6 Bernoulli's method for $x^2 - x - 2 = 0$

i	x_i	$u_i = x_i/x_{i-1}$	$e_i = u_i - s_1$	$|e_i/e_{i-1}|$	$\nabla u_i = u_i - u_{i-1}$	u_i^*
0	3					
1	0					
2	6	∞	∞			
3	6	1	-1.	0		
4	18	3	1.	1.	2	
5	30	1.66667	-0.33	0.33	-1.33333	2.20000
6	66	2.20000	0.20	0.60	0.53333	2.04762
7	126	1.90909	-0.09	0.45	-0.29091	2.01176
8	258	2.04762	0.05	0.53	0.13853	2.00293
9	510	1.97674	-0.023	0.49	-0.07088	2.00073
10	1026	2.01176	0.012	0.51	0.03502	2.00018
11	2046	1.99415	-0.006	0.50	-0.01761	2.00004
12	4098	2.00293	0.003	0.50	0.00878	2.00001
∞		$s_1 = 2.00000$		$|s_2/s_1| = 0.50$		$s_1 = 2.00000$

(4.34) gives

$$x_i = c_1(s_1)^i + c_2(s_2)^i$$

and we may easily verify that in this example (see Section 3.9)

$$c_1 = 1, \quad c_2 = 2, \quad s_1 = 2, \quad s_2 = -1$$

so that

$$x_i = 1(2)^i + 2(-1)^i$$

For large i,

$$x_i \simeq c_1 x_1^i = 2^i$$

and

$$u_i = x_i/x_{i-1} = \frac{2^i + 2(-1)^i}{2^{i-1} + 2(-1)^{i-1}} \simeq \frac{2^i}{2^{i-1}} = 2 \qquad \text{as } i \to \infty.$$

The algorithm and BASIC program for applying Bernoulli's method to a general problem are given below. Although almost any choice of the starting values $x_0, x_1, \ldots, x_{n-1}$ will normally give good results, we must take account of the remote possibility that $c_1 = 0$ in (4.34). This is dealt with by defining $x_0, \ldots, x_{n-1}$ as we have done in part (i) of the algorithm (see Reference 1 for further details).

Algorithm 4.4 Bernoulli's method for a dominant real root s_i

   (i) *Starting values* Set $x_0 = -a_1/a_0$, and define x_i for $i = 1, 2, \ldots, n - 1$, from

$$x_i = - [a_1 x_{i-1} + a_2 x_{i-2} + \cdots + a_i x_0 + (i + 1)a_{i+1}]/a_0$$

(ii) *Recurrence*   Determine x_i for $i = n, n + 1, \ldots$ from

$$x_i = - [a_1 x_{i-1} + a_2 x_{i-2} + \cdots + a_n x_{i-n}]/a_0$$

(iii) *Ratios*   Define u_i for $i = 1, 2, \ldots$ from

$$u_i = x_i/x_{i-1}$$

Then

$$u_i \to s_1 \qquad \text{as } i \to \infty$$

Program 4.4 BERPOL: Bernoulli's method for a polynomial

```
LIST


BERPOL

10 REM- BERPOL : SOLVES POLY EQN A(0)X^N + ... + A(N) =0
20 REM- FINDS DOMINANT REAL SOLUTION BY BERNOULLI'S METHOD
30 REM- NO STARTING VALUES REQUIRED
40 DIM A(10),X(30),U(30)
50 PRINT "DEGREE OF POLYNOMIAL";
60 INPUT N
70 PRINT "POLY COEFFICIENTS A(0),...A(N) (1 PER LINE)"
80 FOR K=0 TO N
90 INPUT A(K)
100 NEXT K
110 PRINT "MAXIMUM NUMBER OF ITERATIONS";
120 INPUT M
130 PRINT "RELATIVE ACCURACY REQUIRED";
140 INPUT E
150 REM- CALCULATES STARTING VALUES X(0),...,X(N-1)
160 X(0)=-A(1)/A(0)
170 U(0)=0
180 I=1
190 IF I>=N GO TO 260
200 C=(I+1)*A(I+1)
210 FOR J=1 TO I
220 C=C+A(J)*X(I-J)
230 NEXT J
240 GO TO 300
250 REM- CALCULATES ITERATES X(N),X(N+1),...
260 C=0
270 FOR J=1 TO N
280 C=C+A(J)*X(I-J)
290 NEXT J
300 X(I)=-C/A(0)
310 U(I)=X(I)/X(I-1)
320 E1=ABS(1-U(I-1)/U(I))
330 IF E1>E GO TO 360
340 PRINT "RELATIVE ACCURACY ATTAINED"
350 GO TO 420
360 IF M>I GO TO 400
370 PRINT "MAXIMUM NUMBER OF ITERATIONS REACHED"
380 GO TO 420
390 REM- UPDATE I
400 I=I+1
410 GO TO 190
420 PRINT " X(I) :        U(I) :"
430 FOR L=0 TO I
440 PRINT X(L),U(L)
450 NEXT L
460 PRINT "APPROX SOLUTION :";U(I)
470 END

Ready

RUN

BERPOL
```

```
DEGREE OF POLYNOMIAL? 3
POLY COEFFICIENTS A(0),...A(N) (1 PER LINE)
? 1
? -10
? -1
? 10.1
MAXIMUM NUMBER OF ITERATIONS? 20
RELATIVE ACCURACY REQUIRED? .0001
RELATIVE ACCURACY ATTAINED
 X(I) :        U(I) :
 10            0
 102           10.2
 999.7         9.80098
 9998          10.001
 99949.5       9.99695
 999396        9.99901
 .999293E+07   9.99897
APPROX SOLUTION : 9.99897
Ready
```

Program notes

(1) It can be seen from the sample run that the numbers $x_1, x_2, \ldots$ can become very large, since each s is approximately s_1 (the largest root) times the previous x. There is therefore a danger of 'accumulator overflow' (i.e. a number occurring outside the computer's range). This may be avoided by 'normalising' the numbers $x_0, x_1, \ldots, x_i$ (at iteration i) by setting

$$x_j := x_j / x_i \qquad (j = 0, \ldots, i)$$

so that in particular the latest x value, namely x_i, is set to unity.
(2) The program will not work if the solution of largest magnitude is complex or if there is more than one solution of largest magnitude (e.g. ± 1).

4.7.2 *Improved convergence*

It is not difficult to verify that, if s_2 is the second largest root of (4.32), then the error e_i between u_i and s_1 is given by

$$e_i = u_i - s_1 \simeq \frac{c_2}{c_1}(s_2 - s_1)\left(\frac{s_2}{s_1}\right)^{i-1} \qquad \text{for large } i.$$

It follows that

$$\left|\frac{e_i}{e_{i-1}}\right| \simeq C = \left|\frac{s_2}{s_1}\right| \qquad \text{for large } i. \qquad (4.35)$$

Since $|s_2| < |s_1|$, we deduce that

$$|e_i| \simeq C\,|e_{i-1}| \qquad \text{where } C < 1.$$

Thus Bernoulli's method is *linear convergent*, and the linear convergence constant is $C = |s_2/s_1|$. This means that the error decreases at a constant rate C. This is verified in Table 4.6 for the quadratic $x^2 - x - 2 = 0$, where the values $|e_i/e_{i-1}|$ can be seen to be converging to

$$0.50 = |-1/2|$$

It has been observed already that linear convergence is not ideal in any algorithm. There are therefore either of the following two choices available to us.

  (i) Use Bernoulli's method to obtain a crude approximation to s_1, and then shift to a rapidly convergent algorithm such as Newton's method or the secant method.
 (ii) Deduce a more accurate value of s_1 based only on the values obtained from Bernoulli's method.

The second alternative is an attractive one, and a suitable technique is in fact available for any linearly convergent algorithm. Full details of its derivation are given by Henrici[1] and the relevant technique is called 'Aitken acceleration', since it is due to A.C. Aitken and effectively speeds up convergence.

4.7.3 Aitken acceleration

For any three consecutive values u_{i-2}, u_{i-1}, u_i of the linearly convergence sequence $\{u_i\}$ we define

$$u_i^* = u_i - \frac{(u_i - u_{i-1})^2}{u_i - 2u_{i-1} + u_{i-2}} \qquad (4.36)$$

then (for i sufficiently large) u_i^* is a better approximation to s_1 than u_i. Specifically it can be shown that, for i large, the errors

$$e_i^* = u_i^* - s_1 \quad \text{and} \quad e_i = u_i - s_1$$

are related by the equation

$$e_i^* \simeq A(e_i)^2 \qquad (4.37)$$

where A is a constant. This means that u_i^* has approximately twice as many correct significant decimal places as u_i, and the calculation of (4.36) has the effect of applying one iteration of a quadratically convergent algorithm.

    Values of u_i^* for $x^2 - x - 2 = 0$ are given in Table 4.6, and the expected improvement on u_i is clearly achieved. For $i = 12$ we deduce that $x_1 \simeq 2.00001$ correct to about 5 decimal places. Moreover it can be verified that

$$e_i^* \simeq 1.33(e_i)^2$$

in Table 4.6 so that (4.37) is realised with $A = 1.33$. It is also clear from Table 4.6 that the sequence of values u_i^* is itself *linearly* convergent. In fact the ratio e_i^*/e_{i-1}^* is approximately 0.25 for i large, which is just the square of the ratio e_i/e_{i-1}. The latter relation is not a coincidence and holds true in general. In summary we thus have the following three general relations between $\{e_i^*\}$ and $\{e_i\}$:

$$\frac{e_i}{e_{i-1}} \simeq C, \quad \frac{e_i^*}{e_{i-1}^*} \simeq C^2, \quad \frac{e_i^*}{(e_i)^2} \simeq A$$

where A and C are constants.

A useful notation, which will be encountered in Chapter 5, is the 'backward difference operator' ∇ defined by

$$\nabla u_i = u_i - u_{i-1} \tag{4.38}$$

The operator ∇^2 may then be defined by:

$$\nabla^2 u_i = \nabla(\nabla u_i) = \nabla(u_i - u_{i-1}) = \nabla u_i - \nabla u_{i-1}$$
$$= (u_i - u_{i-1}) - (u_{i-1} - u_{i-2}) = u_i - 2u_{i-1} + u_{i-2}$$

The formula (4.36) for Aitken acceleration may thus be compactly rewritten as

$$u_i^* = u_i - (\nabla u_i)^2 / \nabla^2 u_i \tag{4.39}$$

For this reason the acceleration method is commonly called the 'Aitken ∇^2-method'.

Note, finally, that the Aitken method can be used in conjunction with *any* linearly convergent sequence (not just the sequence in Bernoulli's method) in order to accelerate convergence. So it could, for example, be used to advantage to speed up the convergence of the fixed-point iteration of Section 4.4 above. (It would *not*, however, be used with the bisection method.)

4.7.4 *Newton's method*

In addition to or as an alternative to the acceleration method above, we may follow up Bernoulli's method for solving (4.32) by a quadratically convergent algorithm such as Newton's method. Once Bernoulli's method has been used to obtain an initial approximation x_0, Newton's method takes the form

$$x_i = g(x_{i-1})$$

where

$$g(x) = x - p_n(x)/p_n'(x).$$

Now Program 3.5 above was designed to evaluate $p_n(x)$ and $p_n'(x)$, and hence only minor changes are needed to convert this program to make it perform Newton's method for a polynomial. The new program, Program 4.5, follows.

Algorithm 4.5 Newton's method for a polynomial $p_n(x)$

(i) Choose x_0 sufficiently close to a required root s.
(ii) For $i = 1, 2, \ldots$, calculate $x_i = g(x_{i-1})$, where $g(x) = x - p_n(x)/p_n'(x)$, using Horner's rule to calculate $p_n(x)$ and $p_n'(x)$. Then $x_i \to s$ as $i \to \infty$.

Program 4.5 NEWPOL: Newton's method for a polynomial

```
LIST


NEWPOL

10 REM- NEWPOL: SOLVES POLY EQN P(X)=A(0)X^N+...+A(N) =0
20 REM- NEWTON'S METHOD: NEEDS STARTING VALUE NEAR SOLUTION
30 DIM A(20),X(30)
40 PRINT "DEGREE OF POLYNOMIAL";
50 INPUT N
60 PRINT "COEFFICIENTS A(0),....,A(N) (1 PER LINE)"
70 FOR K=0 TO N
80 INPUT A(K)
90 NEXT K
100 PRINT "MAXIMUM NUMBER OF ITERATIONS"
110 INPUT M
120 PRINT "RELATIVE ACCURACY REQUIRED";
130 INPUT E
140 PRINT "STARTING VALUE";
150 INPUT X(0)
160 I=1
170 REM- ITERATIONS ON X
180 REM- ACCUMULATES P(X) AND P'(X) IN P AND Q
190 P=A(0)
200 Q=P
210 FOR K=1 TO N
220 P=X(I-1)*P+A(K)
230 IF K=N GO TO 250
240 Q=X(I-1)*Q+P
250 NEXT K
260 E1=-P/Q
270 X(I)=X(I-1)+E1
280 IF ABS(E1/X(I))>E GO TO 340
290 PRINT "RELATIVE ACCURACY ATTAINED "
300 GO TO 370
310 IF M>I GO TO 340
320 PRINT " MAXIMUM NUMBER OF ITERATIONS REACHED"
330 GO TO 370
340 REM- UPDATE I
350 I=I+1
360 GO TO 190
370 PRINT "ITERATED X VALUES :"
380 FOR L=0 TO I
390 PRINT X(L),
400 NEXT L
410 END

Ready

RUN


NEWPOL

DEGREE OF POLYNOMIAL? 3
COEFFICIENTS A(0),....,A(N) (1 PER LINE)
```

```
?  1
?  1
?  1
?  2
MAXIMUM NUMBER OF ITERATIONS
? 10
RELATIVE ACCURACY REQUIRED? .00001
STARTING VALUE? -1
RELATIVE ACCURACY ATTAINED
ITERATED X VALUES :
  -1          -1.5          -1.36842      -1.35339      -1.35321      -1.35321

Ready
```

4.8 Other methods

The discussion above provides a fairly broad introduction to the solution of nonlinear equations. For a more detailed discussion, covering other methods for $f(x) = 0$ (such as Steffensen's method and 'regula falsi'), Newton's method for two nonlinear equations, and methods for complex roots of polynomials, the reader is referred to References 1 and 2.

4.9 References

1. P. Henrici, *Elements of Numerical Analysis*, Wiley, London, (1964)
2. S.D. Conte and C. de Boor, *Elementary Numerical Analysis*, Second Edition, McGraw-Hill, London, (1972)

PROBLEMS

(4.1) Use Program 4.1 (the bisection method) to determine to 3 decimal places the solutions of the following equations:

(a) $x^2 - 4x + 1 = 0$ in $[3, 4]$
(b) $x^3 - x - 1 = 0$ in $[1, 2]$
(c) $2x - \tan x = 0$ in $[1, 1.5]$ (x in radians)

Prove rigorously that the above equations have unique solutions in the specified intervals.

(4.2) The determination of the frequency of vibration of a cantilever beam involves the solution of the equation

$$f(x) = \cos x \cosh x + 2 = 0$$

Prove that this equation has a unique solution s in the range $[0, \pi]$ of x, and determines s to 3 decimal places by the bisection method (Program 4.1). Hint: Sketch $y = \cos x \cosh x$ from $y = \cos x$ and $y = \cosh x$, and see where this intersects $y = -2$.

(4.3) Using Program 4.2 (or by hand), try out the fixed-point iteration $x_i = g(x_{i-1})$ starting from $x_0 = 1.3$ for the solution of the cubic equation

$$x^3 - x - 1 = 0$$

using each of the following iteration functions:

   (a) $g(x) = x^3 - 1$ (b) $g(x) = (x^2 - 1)^{-1}$ (c) $g(x) = (x + 1)^{1/3}$

Determine, by inspection, the limit $|e_i|/|e_{i-1}|$ for any of the iterations which converges, and prove that Criteria 4.2 are satisfied for x in $[1, 2]$. Using (4.23), find an *a posteriori* bound on the error after 4 iterations using the iteration function (c).

Use Aitken acceleration to speed up the convergence of one of the above iterations.

(4.4) A wheel of radius a rolls along the ground at π radians per second. If a point P of the circumference of the wheel is in contact with the ground at time $t = 0$, show that at time t this point P has moved through a horizontal distance

$$s = a(\pi t - \sin \pi t)$$

Show that the time T taken for the point P to move through a given horizontal distance $c\pi a$ is the solution of the nonlinear equation in t:

$$t = g(t) = c + \pi^{-1} \sin \pi t$$

Use Criteria 4.2 to prove that, for any given c in the range $0 < c < \frac{2}{3}$, the fixed-point iteration converges to T for any initial guess t_0 in the range $[c, c + \pi^{-1}]$ of t.

   Calculate T for $c = \frac{1}{4}, \frac{1}{2}, \frac{2}{3}$.

   For $c = \frac{1}{4}$, show that $|g'(t)| \leqslant 1/\sqrt{2}$ and hence, using formula (4.23), obtain an *a posteriori* bound for the error $|t_4 - T|$ after 4 iterations by using the value of t_5.

(4.5) Find suitable fixed-point iterations to solve the following equations. In each case show that Criteria 4.2 are satisfied for the given range of x, and solve the equation to 4 decimal places.

   (a) $x = e^{-x}$ in $[\frac{1}{2}, \ln 2]$
   (b) $x = \tan x$ in $[\pi, 3\pi/2]$
   (c) $e^{-x} = \cos x$ in $[\pi/4, \pi/2]$

Hint: Try $g(x) = \tan x$ and $g(x) = \arctan x$ for (b), and try $g(x) = -\ln \cos x$ and $g(x) = \cos^{-1}(\exp(-x))$ for (c).

(4.6) Extend Program 4.2 so that it calculates, in addition to the set of iterated values x_i, the improved values

$$x_i^* = x_i - \frac{(x_i - x_{i-1})^2}{x_i - 2x_{i-1} + x_{i-2}} \qquad (i \geq 2)$$

obtained by Aitken acceleration, and test this program on the iteration

$$x_i = g(x_{i-1}) \quad \text{for} \quad g(x) = \exp(-x^2), \quad x_0 = 1.$$

(4.7) Write an efficient and reliable program, based on Programs 4.1 and 4.2, which first uses the bisection method to obtain a solution of the given equation $f(x) = 0$ to a specified low relative accuracy ε_1 and then, starting from the value so obtained, uses Newton's method to obtain the solution to a specified high relative accuracy ε_2.

Test this program on the cubic equation

$$x^3 - x - 1 = 0$$

noting that a solution lies in the interval $[1, 2]$ of x.
Hint: You might for example set $\varepsilon_1 = .01$, $\varepsilon_2 = .000001$
(4.8) (i) Test Newton's method (using Program 4.2 or by hand) for finding the square root of a positive number c by solving

$$f(x) = x^2 - c = 0$$

for $c = 2, 3, 5$.
(ii) In the case $c = 2$, show that in the range $[1, \sqrt{2}]$ of x, the iteration function

$$g(x) = x - f(x)/f'(x)$$

has the properties that (a) $g(x)$ increases with x, (b) $|g'(x)| \leq \frac{1}{2}$. Hence prove that Newton's method converges for any x_0 in $[1, \sqrt{2}]$.
Hint: See (4.28) for a formula for $g'(x)$
(4.9) (i) Show that Newton's method for solving the equation

$$f(x) = x^{-1} - c = 0$$

provides an algorithm for calculating the reciprocal of any number c *without division*.

Test this method to determine $1/7$ to 6 decimal places (without divisions) and confirm that the method is quadratically convergent.
(ii) Show that for all positive numbers c, the iteration function

$$g(x) = x - f(x)/f'(x)$$

has the properties in the range $[3c^{-1}/4, c^{-1}]$ of x that (a) $g(x)$

increases with x, (b) $|g'(x)| \leqslant \frac{1}{2}$. Hence prove that Newton's method converges for any x_0 in $[3c^{-1}/4, c^{-1}]$.

(4.10) Test Program 4.3 (the secant method) on any of the examples above. In particular, compare the numbers of iterations required by this method and Newton's method for problems 8 and 9. Do your results confirm that the secant method has an order of convergence of 1.62?

(4.11) Suppose that the secant method is applied to determine the positive solution ($s = 1$) of the equation

$$f(x) = x^2 - 1 = 0$$

By using the formula (4.30) for the iteration, and noting that $e_i = x_i - s = x_i - 1$ and $x_i \simeq 1$, show that for large i

$$e_i \simeq \tfrac{1}{2} e_{i-1} e_{i-2} \qquad (*)$$

By assuming that, for large i,

$$e_i = C(e_{i-1})^p \quad \text{and} \quad e_{i-1} = C(e_{i-2})^p$$

and substituting in $(*)$, deduce that

$$p^2 = p + 1 \quad \text{and} \quad C^p = \tfrac{1}{2}$$

Hence deduce that the iteration has order of convergence $p = (1 + \sqrt{5})/2$.

(4.12) Use Bernoulli's method (Program 4.4) to find to 2 significant figures the solutions of greatest magnitude of each of the following polynomial equations

(a) $x^3 - 10x^2 - x + 10.1 = 0$ (b) $x^2 + 0.1x - 1.1 = 0$

Apply the Aitken acceleration method to obtain improved values of each solution.

Use Newton's method (Program 4.5), starting with the values already obtained above, to determine the relevant solutions of (a) and (b) correct to 6 significant figures.

(4.13) For example (b) of problem 12, determine the linear convergence constant (4.35) of Bernoulli's method, and verify that this is achieved in practice. How many iterations are required to obtain each correct significant figure?

Derive formula (4.35) from (4.34).

(4.14) Write an efficient and reliable program, based on Programs 4.4 and 4.5, to find the real solution of largest magnitude of the polynomial equation (4.32). The program should use Bernoulli's method to obtain a solution of a specified low relative accuracy ε_1, and then proceed to apply Newton's method to obtain a higher relative accuracy ε_2.

Test the program on the examples of problem 12.

Chapter 5

Interpolation, differentiation and integration

ESSENTIAL THEORY

5.1 Introduction

In this chapter we are involved in numerical calculations with functions and data. For a function $y(x)$ defined throughout an interval $[a, b]$ of x, every value of the independent variable x gives a corresponding value of the dependent variable y. However, for a function defined on a discrete set of data ordinates $x_1, x_2 \ldots, x_n$, only the corresponding data abscissae $y_1 = y(x_1), y_2 = y(x_2), \ldots, y_n = y(x_n)$ are known. Although Programs 5.7 to 5.9 below are for convenience designed only for functions defined throughout an interval $[a, b]$, *all* algorithms in the chapter are applicable to functions defined on a discrete set of ordinates and displayed in a table.

For conciseness, the symbol y is used throughout the chapter to denote not only the abscissa but also the name of the function $y(x)$ which generates it.

Three types of calculations are considered. Firstly, the value of $y(x)$ is determined at a given point x which does not appear in the table, and this process is called *interpolation*. Secondly, the value of the gradient $y'(x)$ is calculated at a given point x, which may or may not be an ordinate in the table. Thirdly, the integral $\int_a^b y(x)\, \mathrm{d}x$, namely the area between a and b under the graph of $y = y(x)$, is calculated for two points a and b which may or may not be ordinates in the table.

There are two distinct approaches to these calculations. If many values of the function, gradient, or integral are required, then it is often efficient and convenient to first determine a continuous approximation to the relevant function $y(x)$, $y'(x)$, or $\int y(x)\, \mathrm{d}x$, and then to evaluate this at all required points. The idea is discussed further in Section 5.2. If only a few values are required, then it is normally better to use a method which obtains just one numerical value at a time, and this will be the main subject of the chapter. In methods of this type 'finite differences' prove to be a versatile tool when ordinates are equally spaced, and so an overall discussion of their properties is given prior to these methods.

There is one exception to the general comments above, and that is in the case when many values of an integral are required. Since an integral is calculated numerically by piecing together a number of areas, it is often equally appropriate in this case to use continuous approximation methods as to use finite difference methods. The respective methods are discussed in Sections 5.2 and 5.8.

5.2 Continuous approximation methods

If $y(x)$ is given only as a discrete set of data in a table, then an approximation $y^*(x)$ to $y(x)$ may be obtained by the 'least squares method' in the form of a polynomial or spline[1]. The 'collocation method' might also be used[1], but in the case of polynomials this would only be advisable over a small interval and with a small number of parameters. To interpolate a value of $y(x)$, we then simply evaluate $y^*(x)$ at the appropriate point. This is not an expensive method when many interpolations are required, since each new interpolation only involves an evaluation of $y^*(x)$, and the required number of arithmetic operations is generally proportional to the number of parameters in the approximation.

To calculate $y'(x)$ at many points x (not necessarily in the table) we simply differentiate the approximation $y^*(x)$ and evaluate the resulting function. In the case of a polynomial approximation $y^*(x)$, this calculation has already been coded in Program 3.5. In the case of a 'cubic spline' with 'knots' $\{t_k\}$ of the form

$$y^*(x) = S(x) = c_1 + c_2 x + \cdots + c_4 x^3 + \sum_{k=1}^{n-4} c_{k+4}(x - t_k)_+^3, \quad (5.1)$$

where $(x - t_k)_+^3$ is a notation for the function which is $(x - t_k)^3$ for $x \geq t_k$ and zero for $x < t_k$, the derivative may be calculated in the form

$$S'(x) = c_2 + 2c_3 x + 3c_4 x^2 + 3 \sum_{k=1}^{n-4} c_{k+4}(x - t_k)_+^2 \quad (5.2)$$

(Here $c_1, c_2, \ldots, c_n$ are the parameters in the approximation.) It should be noted, however, that the calculation of a derivative by *any* method is inherently *less accurate* than the calculation of the function itself, and indeed the derivative $y'(x)$ is generally a more badly behaved function than $y(x)$.

The indefinite integral of $y(x)$,

$$z(x) = \int_\alpha^x y(x)\, dx \qquad (\text{for } a \leq \alpha, x \leq b)$$

may be obtained by integrating the approximation $y^*(x)$ to $y(x)$ and choosing a constant of integration so that $z(\alpha) = 0$. In the case of a polynomial approximation of the form

$$y^*(x) = c_1 + c_2 x + \cdots + c_n x^{n-1}$$

we obtain

$$z(x)| \simeq c_1(x - \alpha) + \frac{c_2}{2}(x^2 - \alpha^2) + \frac{c_3}{3}(x^3 - \alpha^3) + \cdots + \frac{c_n}{n}(x^n - \alpha^n) \tag{5.3}$$

Similarly, for the spline function (5.1), we obtain

$$z(x)| \simeq c_1(x - \alpha) + \cdots + \frac{c_4}{4}(x^4 - \alpha^4)$$

$$+ \tfrac{1}{4}\Sigma c_{k+4}\{(x - t_k)_+^4 - (\alpha - t_k)_+^4\} \tag{5.4}$$

The definite integral from a to b may be calculated as

$$\int_a^b y(x)\, dx = \int_\alpha^b y(x)\, dx - \int_\alpha^a y(x)\, dx = z(b) - z(a) \tag{5.5}$$

Note that, in contrast to $y'(x)$, the integral of $y(x)$ is typically more accurately determined than $y(x)$ itself, since integration is a smoothing process. So we can aim for numerical results which are at least as accurate as the data.

We now turn to methods designed to interpolate, differentiate, or integrate at *one* point only, and we start by interpolating in a table, when the ordinate spacing is not assumed to be uniform.

5.3 Interpolation with unequally spaced ordinates

The interpolation methods in the remainder of the chapter have the effect of collocating a polynomial of degree n to known function values $y_i = y(x_i)$ at a set of ordinates x_i ($i = 1, \ldots, n$), and then evaluating this polynomial at the required point x. (We advise the reader that we use the word 'interpolate' to mean 'determine a function value at a point between data ordinates', and the word 'collocate' to mean 'match abscissae exactly'.)

A simple formula, called the Lagrange interpolation formula, interpolates a value of $y(x)$ at the point x as follows:

$$y(x) \simeq p(x) = \sum_{i=1}^{n} y(x_i) l_i(x) \tag{5.6}$$

where

$$l_i(x) = \prod_{\substack{j=1 \\ j \neq i}}^{n} \frac{x - x_j}{x_i - x_j}$$

$$= \frac{(x - x_1)(x - x_2) \ldots (x - x_{i-1})(x - x_{i+1}) \ldots (x - x_n)}{(x_i - x_1)(x_i - x_2) \ldots (x_i - x_{i-1})(x_i - x_{i+1}) \ldots (x_i - x_n)} \quad (5.7)$$

and $\{x_i\}$ are chosen data ordinates for collocation. Here the notation

$$\prod_{\substack{j=1 \\ j \neq i}}^{n} \quad \text{or more briefly} \quad \prod_{j \neq i}$$

denotes a product over the values $j = 1$ to n, but excluding $j = i$. For example

$$\prod_{\substack{j=1 \\ j \neq 2}}^{4} c_j = c_1 c_3 c_4$$

It is easy to verify that $p(x)$ given by (5.6) is indeed the polynomial of degree $n - 1$ which collocates $y(x)$ at $x_1, \ldots, x_n$. Firstly, (5.6) is a polynomial of degree $n - 1$, as indeed are each of the functions $l_i(x)$. Secondly, for any of the points $x = x_k$ $(k = 1, \ldots, n)$, it is clear that

$$l_i(x_k) = \begin{cases} 0 & \text{for } i \neq k \\ 1 & \text{for } i = k \end{cases} \quad (5.8)$$

and hence

$$p(x_k) = \sum_{i=1}^{n} y(x_i) l_i(x_k) = y(x_k)$$

The use of (5.6) and (5.7) to calculate the interpolated value $p(x)$ for $y(x)$ is very straightforward, and the algorithm and program are as follows. (Note that the calculation of a product was covered in Program 3.1A.)

Algorithm 5.1 Lagrange interpolation formula based on n *points*

(i) Specify n ordinates $x_1, \ldots, x_n$ and corresponding function values $y_1 = y(x_1), y_2 = y(x_2), \ldots, y_n = y(x_n)$.
(ii) Specify each point x at which a value $y(x)$ is to be interpolated.
(iii) Calculate $y(x)$ from the formulae (5.6) and (5.7).

Program 5.1 LAGINT: Lagrange interpolation formula

```
LIST
LAGINT

10       REM- LAGINT: CALCULATES Y(X) FROM VALUES Y(X(1)),...,Y(X(N))
20       REM- AT X(1),...,X(N) BY LAGRANGE INTERPOLATION FORMULA.
30       REM- Y(I) DENOTES Y(X(I)), Z DENOTES PT OF INTERPOLATION.
40       DIM X(20),Y(20)
50       PRINT "NO OF COLLOCATION PTS";
60       INPUT N
70       PRINT "DATA X,Y(X) AT INTERPOLATION PTS"
80       FOR I=1 TO N
90       INPUT X(I),Y(I)
100      NEXT I
110      GO TO 150
120      PRINT "INPUT 0 TO STOP, 1 TO INTERPOLATE AGAIN";
130      INPUT A
140      IF A=0 THEN 280
150      PRINT "POINT X FOR INTERPOLATION";
160      INPUT Z
170      F=0
180      FOR I=1 TO N
190      C=1
200      FOR J=1 TO N
210      IF J=I THEN 230
220      C=C*(Z-X(J))/(X(I)-X(J))
230      NEXT J
240      F=F+C*Y(I)
250      NEXT I
260      PRINT "INTERPOLATED VALUE:",F
270      GO TO 120
280      END

Ready

RUN
LAGINT

NO OF COLLOCATION PTS? 5
DATA X,Y(X) AT INTERPOLATION PTS
?   0, 0
?  .1,.0998334
?  .3,.29552
?  .6,.564642
?  .9,.783327
POINT X FOR INTERPOLATION? .5236
INTERPOLATED VALUE:          .49999
INPUT 0 TO STOP, 1 TO INTERPOLATE AGAIN? 1
POINT X FOR INTERPOLATION? .7854
INTERPOLATED VALUE:          .707149
INPUT 0 TO STOP, 1 TO INTERPOLATE AGAIN? 0
Ready
```

Program notes

(1) At the end of the calculation, control is returned to statement 120, so that a new point of interpolation x (i.e. Z in the program) can be input.

(2) The program is tested on some data from the function $y = \sin x$, to interpolate at $x = \pi/6, \pi/4$.

5.3.1 *Successive interpolation*

Often, after performing interpolation by collocation at a set of points $x_1, \ldots, x_n$, we wish to repeat the process for a larger set of collocation points $x_1, \ldots, x_{n+1}$ using a polynomial of higher degree n. In this way results can be compared and the accuracy of $y(x)$

estimated. However, there is a simple and very efficient algorithm for determining a succession of collocation polynomials, which uses more and more collocation points. It is called *Neville's Algorithm*.

Suppose that $P_{ir}(x)$ is the polynomial of degree r which collocates $y(x)$ at $x_{i-r}, x_{i-r+1}, \ldots, x_{i-1}, x_i$, where $x_1, \ldots, x_m$ is the *complete* set of ordinates for the data and $y_i = y(x_i)$ $(i = 1, \ldots, m)$ are the corresponding function values. Then

$$\left. \begin{array}{l} P_{i0}(x) = y_i \\[2mm] P_{ir}(x) = \dfrac{(x_i - x)P_{i-1,r-1}(x) - (x_{i-r} - x)P_{i,r-1}(x)}{x_i - x_{i-r}} \end{array} \right\} \quad (5.9)$$

where $i = 1, \ldots, m$; $r = 0, 1, \ldots, m - 1$. The proof of this formula is left as an exercise to the reader (Problem 3).

The formula (5.9) determines the polynomial collocating $y(x)$ at $x_{i-r}, \ldots, x_i$ from two polynomials of one degree less collocating at $x_{i-r}, \ldots, x_{i-1}$ and $x_{i-r+1}, \ldots, x_i$, respectively. For example, for $i = 3$ and $r = 2$, the polynomial $P_{32}(x)$ of degree 2 collocating at x_1, x_2, x_3 is defined in terms of two polynomials of degree 1, $P_{21}(x)$ collocating at x_1, x_2 and $P_{31}(x)$ collocating at x_2, x_3. In Table 5.1 we give a tableau which illustrates the calculation of these polynomials, with arrows to indicate the progress of the calculation. It is clear that we must determine one column of the tableau at a time.

Table 5.1 Progression of Neville's algorithm

r	0	1	2	3	$\cdots$
x_1	$y_1 = P_{10}$				
x_2	$y_2 = P_{20}$	P_{21}			
x_3	$y_3 = P_{30}$	P_{31}	P_{32}		
x_4	$y_4 = P_{40}$	P_{41}	P_{42}	P_{43}	

The following formal algorithm and program adopt Neville's algorithm to interpolate $y(x)$ at a given x by evaluating $P_{t,t-s}(x)$, the polynomial of degree $t - s$ which collates $y(x)$ at the points x_s, $x_{s+1}, \ldots, x_t$ (amongst the ordinates $x_1, \ldots, x_m$). It also calculates all polynomials collocating on smaller sets of consecutive points from $x_s, \ldots, x_t$ (which are used by the algorithm).

Algorithm 5.2 *Neville's algorithm based on points* $x_s, \ldots, x_t$

(i) Specify *m* ordinates $x_1, \ldots, x_m$ and corresponding function values $y_1 = y(x_1), \ldots, y_m = y(x_m)$.

(ii) Specify a point *x* at which $y(x)$ is to be evaluated.

(iii) Specify the indices *s* and *t* of the first and last collocation ordinates.

(iv) Determine an array of polynomials $P_{ir}(x)$ which collocate at $x_{i-r}, \ldots, x_i$, by applying Neville's algorithm (5.9) only for $i = s + r, \ldots, t$ and $r = 1, \ldots, t - s$.

Program 5.2 NEVINT: Neville's interpolation algorithm

```
LIST
NEVINT

10      REM- NEVINT: CALCULATES Y(X) FROM VALUES Y(X(S)),...,Y(X(T))
20      REM- BY NEVILLE'S ALGORITHM. P(I,R) IS VALUE AT X OF POLY
30      REM- OF DEGREE R INTERPOLATING Y AT X(I),...,X(I-R).
40      REM- PRINTS OUT P(I,R) FOR I=S+R TO T WHILE R=1 TO N.
50      REM- BEST ANSWER IS LAST P : P(T,N). (N=T-S)
60      REM- Z DENOTES X, Y(I) DENOTES Y(X(I)).
70      DIM P(10,10),X(10),Y(10)
80      PRINT "NO OF DATA PTS";
90      INPUT M
100     PRINT "DATA X,Y :"
110     FOR I=1 TO M
120     INPUT X(I),Y(I)
130     NEXT I
140     GO TO 180
150     PRINT "INPUT 0 TO STOP, 1 TO INTERPOLATE AGAIN"
160     INPUT A
170     IF A=0 THEN 360
180     PRINT "POINT X FOR INTERPOLATING Y(X)";
190     INPUT Z
200     PRINT "INDICES OF 1ST & LAST INTERPOLN PTS"
210     INPUT S,T
220     N=T-S
230     REM- POLY OF DEGREE 0 GIVEN BY Y(X(I))
240     FOR I=S TO T
250     P(I,0)=Y(I)
260     NEXT I
270     REM- POLYS OF DEGREE R=1,...,N
280     FOR R=1 TO N
290     PRINT "INTERPOLN POLY OF DEGREE";R
300     FOR I=S+R TO T
310     P(I,R)=((X(I)-Z)*P(I-1,R-1)-(X(I-R)-Z)*P(I,R-1))/(X(I)-X(I-R))
320     PRINT P(I,R)
330     NEXT I
340     NEXT R
350     GO TO 150
360     END

Ready




RUN
NEVINT

NO OF DATA PTS? 7
DATA X,Y :
? -.1,-.0998334
?  0, 0
? .1,.0998334
? .3,.29552
? .6,.564642
? .9,.783327
? 1,.841471
POINT X FOR INTERPOLATING Y(X)? .5236
INDICES OF 1ST & LAST INTERPOLN PTS
? 2,6
```

```
INTERPOLN POLY OF DEGREE 1
 .522728
 .514298
 .496106
 .50895
INTERPOLN POLY OF DEGREE 2
 .508014
 .498885
 .500892
INTERPOLN POLY OF DEGREE 3
 .500048
 .499948
INTERPOLN POLY OF DEGREE 4
 .49999
INPUT 0 TO STOP, 1 TO INTERPOLATE AGAIN
? 1
POINT X FOR INTERPOLATING Y(X)? .7854
INDICES OF 1ST & LAST INTERPOLN PTS
? 1,7
INTERPOLN POLY OF DEGREE 1
 .784091
 .784091
 .770451
 .730959
 .699789
 .716694
INTERPOLN POLY OF DEGREE 2
 .784092
 .748381
 .716316
 .705743
 .707625
INTERPOLN POLY OF DEGREE 3
 .705047
 .706407
 .707257
 .707048
INTERPOLN POLY OF DEGREE 4
 .706768
 .707149
 .707098
INTERPOLN POLY OF DEGREE 5
 .707106
 .707109
INTERPOLN POLY OF DEGREE 6
 .707108
INPUT 0 TO STOP, 1 TO INTERPOLATE AGAIN
? 0
Ready
```

Program notes

(1) One column of the Neville tableau is output at a time (compare Table 5.1) under the heading 'interpoln poly of degree r' (for $r = 1, 2, 3, \ldots$). For example, the first printed entry, namely $P_{s+r,r}$, collocates at $x_s, \ldots, x_{s+r}$. (If $s = 1$, this is a diagonal entry in Table 5.1.) The set of these first entries collocate, respectively, in the sets $\{x_s, x_{s+1}\}, \{x_s, x_{s+1}, x_{s+2}\}, \ldots, \{x_s, x_{s+1}, \ldots, x_t\}$.

(2) The program is tested on data of $y = \sin x$, using up to 5 points to interpolate at $x = \pi/6$ and up to 7 points to interpolate at $x = \pi/4$.

5.4 Finite differences and their applications

Turning now to tables with equally spaced ordinates, the study of 'finite differences' leads to a unified approach for obtaining a wide variety of numerical methods for interpolation, differentiation and integration.

Suppose that

$$\{x_i\} \qquad (i = \cdots, -2, -1, 0, 1, 2, \ldots)$$

are equally spaced ordinates at steps of h along the x axis (see Figure 5.1). Then

$$x_i = x_0 + ih$$

for all integers i. Let us also include points x between the ordinates by defining

$$x_p = x_0 + ph \qquad \text{for all real numbers } p. \tag{5.10}$$

For example the point midway between x_0 and x_1 is $x_{1/2}$ (or $x_{.5}$) and we may even refer to a point such as $x_{1.372}$, which is .372 of the way between x_1 to x_2. The abscissae, or y values, are given corresponding indexed values

$$y_p = y(x_p) \tag{5.11}$$

for all real p.

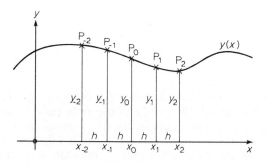

Figure 5.1 Ordinates and abscissae

Many problems involve derivatives of $y(x)$, and standard numerical methods express these approximately in terms of differences of function values at ordinates. For example $y'(x_1)$, which is $y'(x)$ evaluated at the ordinate x_1, may be approximated in any of the following three ways:

$$y'(x_1) \simeq \frac{y(x_2) - y(x_1)}{x_2 - x_1} = \frac{y_2 - y_1}{h}$$

$$y'(x_1) \simeq \frac{y(x_1) - y(x_0)}{x_1 - x_0} = \frac{y_1 - y_0}{h} \qquad (5.12)$$

$$y'(x_1) \simeq \frac{y(x_2) - y(x_0)}{x_2 - x_0} = \frac{y_2 - y_0}{2h}$$

These approximations are in fact the gradients of the chords P_1P_2, P_0P_1, P_0P_2, respectively, which join up pairs of points on $y = y(x)$ (see Figure 5.1). The formulae (5.12) may be expressed neatly by introducing 'finite difference operators'.

5.4.1 *Finite difference operators and the shift operator*

Define the *forward difference operator* Δ, *backward difference operator* ∇, and *central difference operator* δ by the relations:

$$\Delta y_i = y_{i+1} - y_i, \quad \nabla y_i = y_i - y_{i-1}, \quad \delta y_i = y_{i+1/2} - y_{i-1/2} \quad (5.13)$$

Then Δy_i, ∇y_i, δy_i are numerical values, which are referred to as the forward, backward, and central differences of y at x_i. Each of these differences is obtained by subtracting two y values at ordinates spaced h apart.

Note that δy_i involves y values at 'half points' which do not appear in the data, and so we generally prefer in practice to use the difference $y_{i+1} - y_{i-1}$ at ordinates spaced $2h$ apart. This difference may be expressed in terms of δ, if we introduce a new operator μ called the *mean value operator*:

$$\mu y_i = \tfrac{1}{2}(y_{i+1/2} + y_{i-1/2}) \qquad (5.14)$$

All the operators Δ, ∇, δ, μ may be 'multiplied' in an obvious way, and in particular the *mean central difference operator* $\mu\delta$ is given by

$$(\mu\delta)y_i = \mu(\delta y_i) = \mu(y_{i+1/2} - y_{i-1/2}) = \mu y_{i+1/2} - \mu y_{i-1/2}$$
$$= \tfrac{1}{2}(y_{i+1} + y_i) - \tfrac{1}{2}(y_i + y_{i-1}) = \tfrac{1}{2}(y_{i+1} - y_{i-1})$$

Thus

$$2\mu\delta y_i = y_{i+1} - y_{i-1} \qquad (5.15)$$

Clearly the approximations (5.12) may now be abbreviated as

$$y_1' \simeq h^{-1} \Delta y_1, \quad y_1' \simeq h^{-1} \nabla y_1, \quad y_1' \simeq h^{-1} \mu\delta y_1$$

and more generally we have the approximations

$$y_i' \simeq h^{-1} \Delta y_i, \quad y_i' \simeq h^{-1} \nabla y_i, \quad y_i' \simeq h^{-1} \mu\delta y_i \qquad (5.16)$$

The approximations (5.16) involve 'first order' differences. However, we may also define higher orders of differences as follows.

$$\Delta^2 y_i = \Delta(\Delta y_i) = \Delta(y_{i+1} - y_i) = \Delta y_{i+1} - \Delta y_i$$
$$= (y_{i+2} - y_{i+1}) - (y_{i+1} - y_i)$$

Thus

$$\left. \begin{array}{l} \Delta^2 y_i = y_{i+2} - 2y_{i+1} + y_i \\ \nabla^2 y_i = y_i - 2y_{i-1} + y_{i-2}, \quad \delta^2 y_i = y_{i+1} - 2y_i + y_{i-1} \end{array} \right\} \quad (5.17)$$

Similarly

Note that, unlike δy_i, $\delta^2 y_i$ involves proper data ordinates, and so there is no need to use the operator μ with it. By analogy with (5.16) we may write

$$y_i'' \simeq h^{-2} \Delta^2 y_i, \quad y_i'' \simeq h^{-2} \nabla^2 y_i, \quad y_i'' \simeq h^{-2} \delta^2 y_i \quad (5.18)$$

so that the second order differences provide rough approximations to the second derivative. Similarly we can define higher order differences $\Delta^3 y_i$, $\Delta^4 y_i$, ...; $\nabla^3 y_i$, $\nabla^4 y_i$, ...; $\mu \delta^3 y_i$, $\delta^4 y_i$, $\mu \delta^5 y_i$, $\delta^6 y_i$, ..., which relate to higher order derivatives of y at $x = x_i$. Note that mean central differences need to be used in place of central differences for all *odd* orders of δ.

There is a simple connection between μ and δ, which is useful as a means of introducing μ when it is needed.

$$\mu^2 y_i = \mu(\mu y_i) = \mu(\tfrac{1}{2} y_{i+1/2} + \tfrac{1}{2} y_{i-1/2}) = \tfrac{1}{4}(y_{i+1} + y_i) + \tfrac{1}{4}(y_i + y_{i-1})$$
$$= \tfrac{1}{4}(y_{i+1} + 2y_i + y_{i-1}) = \tfrac{1}{4}(\delta^2 y_i + 4y_i)$$
$$= (1 + \tfrac{1}{4}\delta^2)y_i \quad \text{from (5.17)}$$

Hence

$$\mu^2 = 1 + \tfrac{1}{4} \delta^2 \quad (5.19)$$

In fact all of the operators Δ, ∇, μ, δ may be interlinked, and in particular each may be expressed conveniently in terms of a single new operator E, called the *shift operator*, which is defined by the relation

$$E y_i = y_{i+1} \quad (5.20)$$

and simply adds 1 to the index of y, or, equivalently, moves to the next abscissa. A logical extension of (5.20) follows by obvious algebraic operations:

$$E^2 y_i = E(E y_i) = E y_{i+1} = y_{i+2}, \quad E^3 y_i = E E^2 y_i = E y_{i+2} = y_{i+3}, \text{ etc}$$

In general

$$E^k y_i = y_{i+k}$$

for any integers k, i. This formula also applies for negative k, since the operator E^{-1} (the inverse of the operator E) then satisfies

$$E^{-1}Ey_i = E^{-1}y_{i+1} = y_i,$$

so that

$$E^{-1}E = 1.$$

Indeed by an obvious generalisation we may define

$$E^p y_q = y_{q+p} \tag{5.21}$$

for *any real* numbers p and q.

From (5.13), (5.14), (5.15), and (5.21) we deduce the links between Δ, ∇, μ, δ and E:

$$\Delta y_i = Ey_i - y_i = (E - 1)y_i$$
$$\Rightarrow \Delta = E - 1 \tag{5.22}$$

$$\nabla y_i = y_i - E^{-1}y_i = (1 - E^{-1})y_i$$
$$\Rightarrow \nabla = 1 - E^{-1} \tag{5.23}$$

$$\delta y_i = E^{1/2}y_i - E^{-1/2}y_i = (E^{1/2} - E^{-1/2})y_i$$
$$\Rightarrow \delta = E^{1/2} - E^{-1/2} \tag{5.24}$$

$$\mu y_i = \tfrac{1}{2}(E^{1/2}y_i + E^{-1/2}y_i) = \tfrac{1}{2}(E^{1/2} + E^{-1/2})y_i$$
$$\Rightarrow \mu = \tfrac{1}{2}(E^{1/2} + E^{-1/2}) \tag{5.25}$$

$$\mu\delta y_i = \tfrac{1}{2}(Ey_i - E^{-1}y_i) = \tfrac{1}{2}(E - E^{-1})y_i$$
$$\Rightarrow \mu\delta = \tfrac{1}{2}(E - E^{-1}) \tag{5.26}$$

5.4.2 *Difference tables*

Finite differences are very simple to use, especially when they are displayed in tables. The actual entries that occur in forward, backward, and central difference tables are shown in Tables 5.2, 5.3, 5.4 below. Algebraic names are used for the entries in these tables, whereas numerical values would occur in a practical example. In the case of central differences, we have inserted (in square brackets) extra columns to include the mean central differences $\mu\delta y_i$, $\mu\delta^3 y_i, \ldots$, of odd order in δ. The ordinary central differences of odd order correspond to the half points $x_{0.5}, x_{1.5}, x_{2.5}, x_{3.5}, \ldots$ which are bracketed in Table 5.4 since they are not actually ordinates.

Table 5.2 Entries in a forward difference table

x_0	y_0	Δy_0	$\Delta^2 y_0$	$\Delta^3 y_0$	$\Delta^4 y_0$	$\ldots$
x_1	y_1	Δy_1	$\Delta^2 y_1$	$\Delta^3 y_1$	$\vdots$	
x_2	y_2	Δy_2	$\Delta^2 y_2$	$\vdots$		
x_3	y_3	Δy_3	$\vdots$			
x_4	y_4	$\vdots$				
$\vdots$	$\vdots$					

Table 5.3 Entries in a backward difference table

x_0	y_0					
x_1	y_1	∇y_1				
x_2	y_2	∇y_2	$\nabla^2 y_2$			
x_3	y_3	∇y_3	$\nabla^2 y_3$	$\nabla^3 y_3$		
x_4	y_4	∇y_4	$\nabla^2 y_4$	$\nabla^3 y_4$	$\nabla^4 y_4$	$\ldots$
$\vdots$	$\vdots$	$\vdots$	$\vdots$	$\vdots$	$\vdots$	

Table 5.4 Entries in a central difference table

x_0	y_0						
$(x_{0.5})$		$\delta y_{0.5}$					
x_1	y_1		$\left[\mu\delta y_1 \right.$	$\delta^2 y_1$			
$(x_{1.5})$		$\delta y_{1.5}$			$\delta^3 y_{1.5}$		
x_2	y_2		$\mu\delta y_2$	$\delta^2 y_2$		$[\mu\delta^3 y_2]$	$\delta^4 y_2 \quad \ldots$
$(x_{2.5})$		$\delta y_{2.5}$			$\delta^3 y_{2.5}$	$\vdots$	$\vdots$
x_3	y_3		$\left. \mu\delta y_3 \right]$	$\delta^2 y_3$	$\vdots$		
$(x_{3.5})$		$\delta y_{3\,5}$	$\vdots$	$\vdots$			
x_4	y_4	$\vdots$					
$\vdots$	$\cdot$						

To illustrate how tables work out for a numerical example, we give in Tables 5.5 to 5.7 all relevant entries to 4 decimals for the function $y = e^x$ with ordinates $1.0, 1.1, \ldots, 1.4$. The calculation is very straightforward; each entry is obtained by taking the difference of an appropriate pair of adjacent values in the previous column. The mean central differences $\mu\delta y_i$, $\mu\delta^3 y_i$, $\ldots$ in Table 5.7 are obtained by taking the mean of a pair of adjacent entries in the previous column.

Table 5.5 Forward differences of $y = e^x$ at 1.0, 1.1, ... , 1.4

i	x_i	y_i	Δy_i	$\Delta^2 y_i$	$\Delta^3 y_i$	$\Delta^4 y_i$
0	1.0	2.7183	0.2859	0.0300	0.0033	0.0001
1	1.1	3.0042	0.3159	0.0333	0.0034	
2	1.2	3.3201	0.3492	0.0367		
3	1.3	3.6693	0.3859			
4	1.4	4.0552				

Table 5.6 Backward differences of $y = e^x$ at 1.0, 1.1, ... 1.4

i	x_i	y_i	∇y_i	$\nabla^2 y_i$	$\nabla^3 y_i$	$\nabla^4 y_i$
0	1.0	2.7183				
1	1.1	3.0042	0.2859			
2	1.2	3.3201	0.3159	0.0300		
3	1.3	3.6693	0.3492	0.0333	0.0033	
4	1.4	4.0552	0.3859	0.0367	0.0034	0.0001

Table 5.7 Central differences of $y = e^x$ at 1.0, 1.1, ... , 1.4

i	x_i	y_i	δy_i	$[\mu\delta y_i]$	$\delta^2 y_i$	$\delta^3 y_i$	$[\mu\delta^3 y_i]$	$\delta^4 y_i$
0	1.0	2.7183						
(0.5)	(1.05)		0.2859					
1	1.1	3.0042		0.3009	0.0300			
(1.5)	(1.15)		0.3159			0.0033		
2	1.2	3.3201		0.3326	0.0333		[0.0033]	0.0001
(2.5)	(1.25)		0.3492			0.0034		
3	1.3	3.669?		0.3676	0.0367			
(3.5)	(1.35)		0.3859					
4	1.4	4.0552						

On studying Tables 5.5, 5.6, 5.7, various features come to our notice. Firstly, the actual numerical entries (apart from the mean central differences in square brackets) are *identical* in all 3 tables, and tables only differ in the placings of the numbers. Indeed we can in general write

$$\Delta y_i = \nabla y_{i+1} = \delta y_{i+1/2} \qquad (5.27)$$

Secondly, the numbers decrease in magnitude from left and right, and this is a feature typical of 'nice' functions which may be smoothly differentiated as often as required. Indeed, by applying (5.16) repetitively, we have for sufficiently small h the approximations

$$\frac{\mathrm{d}^k y_i}{\mathrm{d}x^k} \simeq h^{-k} \, \Delta^k y_i \simeq h^{-k} \, \nabla^k y_i \simeq h^{-k} \, \delta^k y_i$$

so that $\Delta^k y_i$, $\nabla^k y_i$, and $\delta^k y_i$ are approximately proportional to h^k. If we use the *order notation* $O(h^k)$ to denote a series of form

$$c_k h^k + c_{k+1} h^{k+1} + \cdots$$

starting with a term in h^k, then precise relations are obtained:

$$\Delta^k y_i = O(h^k), \quad \nabla^k y_i = O(h^k), \quad \delta^k y_i = O(h^k) \qquad (5.28)$$

For $h = 0.1$, for example, Δy_0, $\Delta^2 y_0$, $\Delta^3 y_0$, ... are roughly proportional to $.1$, $.1^2$, $.1^3$, ... according to (5.28), and this is confirmed in Table 5.5. The relations (5.28) provide a simple but valuable tool in assessing *truncation error* for methods based on finite differences.

In addition to truncation error, we must also consider *rounding error*, and in fact this grows rather rapidly in finite difference tables. For example, in Table 5.8, we show the actual entries produced when small errors ε, $-\varepsilon$, ε, $-\varepsilon$, ε are respectively added to the data $y_0, \ldots, y_4$ of Table 5.2. And in Table 5.9, the calculation is performed with $\varepsilon = .0001$ using the numerical values of Table 5.5.

Table 5.8 Rounding errors of $\pm\varepsilon$ in Table 5.2

$y_0 + \varepsilon$	$\Delta y_0 - 2\varepsilon$	$\Delta^2 y_0 + 4\varepsilon$	$\Delta^3 y_0 - 8\varepsilon$	$\Delta^4 y_0 + 16\varepsilon$
$y_1 - \varepsilon$	$\Delta y_1 + 2\varepsilon$	$\Delta^2 y_1 - 4\varepsilon$	$\Delta^3 y_1 + 8\varepsilon$	
$y_2 + \varepsilon$	$\Delta y_2 - 2\varepsilon$	$\Delta^2 y_2 + 4\varepsilon$		
$y_3 - \varepsilon$	$\Delta y_3 + 2\varepsilon$			
$y_4 + \varepsilon$				

Table 5.9 Rounding errors of $\pm.0001$ in Table 5.5

i	y_i	Δy_i	$\Delta^2 y_i$	$\Delta^3 y_i$	$\Delta^4 y_i$
0	2.7184	.2857	.0304	.0025	.0017
1	3.0041	.3161	.0329	.0042	
2	3.3202	.3490	.0371		
3	3.6692	.3861			
4	4.0553				

Note that the entry $\Delta^4 y_0$ is very different in Table 5.9 from that in Table 5.5. Clearly any rounding error that occurs at any stage is propagated as differences are formed, and so the calculation is actually *unstable*. This means in practice that we *must not use too many columns of differences*. Specifically a rounding error becomes up to 2^p times as large after p columns have been calculated, or in other words one decimal place of absolute accuracy is lost for every $\log_{10} 2$ (about 3.3) columns of differences calculated.

When we come to make use of difference tables, we often require entries from only one row of the table, corresponding to a given ordinate x_i. We can therefore draw further conclusions from Tables 5.5–5.7. Firstly, we typically use forward, backward, or central difference tables according as the ordinate x_i is at the top, bottom, or middle of the table. This is particularly true, as we shall see in the case of formulae for differentiation. Secondly, although the main entries in Tables 5.5, 5.6, 5.7 are identical, we use different combinations of entries for particular ordinates.

The forward difference entries at x_0 in Table 5.5 are y_0, Δy_0, $\Delta^2 y_0, \ldots$, the backward difference entries at x_4 are y_4, Δy_3, $\Delta^2 y_2, \ldots$ (namely the 'outside' entries in Table 5.5), and the central difference entries y_2, $\delta^2 y_2$, $\delta^4 y_2, \ldots$ at x_2 are y_2, $\Delta^2 y_1$, $\Delta^4 y_0, \ldots$ (i.e. the numbers 3.3201, 0.0333, 0.0001, ... in Table 5.5, which are obtained by making 'knight's moves' up the data). The mean central differences $\mu\delta y_2$, $\mu\delta^3 y_2, \ldots$ have to be calculated separately if they are required.

We now give an algorithm and program to generate both forward and mean central difference tables. The forward difference table consists of an array with entries $d_{ik} \equiv \Delta^k y_i$ in row i and column k. Each column is calculated from the previous one by the relation

$$d_{ik} = d_{i+1,k-1} - d_{i,k-1} \qquad (5.29)$$

which expresses the fact that

$$\Delta^k y_i = \Delta(\Delta^{k-1} y_i) = \Delta^{k-1} y_{i+1} - \Delta^{k-1} y_i$$

Once the forward difference table has been generated, then both backward and central difference tables may be deduced by rearrangement (according to (5.27)). The mean central differences, namely the entries in square brackets in Table 5.4, are generated as an array of entries c_{jl} (in row j, column l) numbered according to their occurrence. Thus j is the index of the x ordinate, and k is $2l - 1$, where k is the (odd) order of differences ($l = 1, 2, \ldots$). It is easy to verify from (5.27) that

$$c_{i+l,l} = \mu\delta^{2l-1} y_{i+l} = \mu\Delta^k y_{i+1/2} = \tfrac{1}{2}(\Delta^k y_{i+1} + \Delta^k y_i) \qquad (5.30)$$

Hence

$$c_{i+l,l} = \tfrac{1}{2}(d_{i+1,k} + d_{ik}), \quad \text{where} \quad k = 2l - 1 \qquad (5.31)$$

For example from Tables 5.5 and 5.7 the relevant values are as follows.

$$\underline{l = 1}$$

$$i = 0: \ c_{11} = \mu\delta y_1 = .3099$$
$$i = 1: \ c_{21} = \mu\delta y_2 = .3326$$
$$i = 2: \ c_{31} = \mu\delta y_3 = .3676$$

$$\underline{l = 2}$$

$$i = 0: \ c_{22} = \mu\delta^3 y_2 = .0033$$

Algorithm 5.3 Tables of forward differences and mean central differences

(i) Specify x_0 and h, and the number m of ordinates after x_0. Calculate $x_1, \ldots, x_m$ from (5.10).

(ii) Specify abscissae $y_0, \ldots, y_m$, and the maximum order $n(\leqslant m)$ of differences required.

(iii) Calculate forward differences $d_{ik} = \Delta^k y_i$ from (5.29) for $k = 1, \ldots, n$ and $i = 0, \ldots, m - k$, where $d_{i0} = y_i$.

(iv) Calculate mean central differences $c_{i+l,l} = \mu\delta^{2l-1}y_{i+l}$ from (5.31) for $i = 0, 1, \ldots, r$, and for all l such that $k = 2l - 1$ and $k \leqslant n$, where $r = m - k - 1$.

(v) Print out tables of d_{ik} and c_{jl} in their 'natural' positions.

Program 5.3 TABDIF: Tables of finite differences

```
LIST
TABDIF

10      REM- TABDIF: CALCULATES TABLES OF FORWARD AND MEAN CENTRAL
20      REM- DIFFERENCES FOR A SET OF DATA (X,Y).
30      REM- D(I,K) IS ORDER K FORWARD DIFFCE AT X(I).
40      REM- C(I,K) IS MEAN ORDER K CENTRAL DIFFCE AT X(I).
50      MARGIN 70
60      DIM X(10),Y(10),D(10,10),C(10,10)
70      PRINT "NO OF DATA PTS LESS 1";
80      INPUT M
90      PRINT "FIRST DATA POINT, X STEP";
100     INPUT X(0),H
110     FOR I=1 TO M
120     X(I)=X(I-1)+H
130     NEXT I
140     PRINT "Y VALUES"
150     FOR I=0 TO M
160     INPUT Y(I)
170     D(I,0)=Y(I)
180     NEXT I
190     PRINT "NO OF COLUMNS OF DIFFERENCES";
200     INPUT N
```

```
210     REM- CALCULATES FORWARD DIFFERENCES: K=COL, I=ROW
220     REM- CALCULATES ODD ORDER MEAN CENTRAL DIFFERENCES:
230     REM- A>0 IMPLIES THAT K IS ODD, L= COLUMN COUNTER
240     REM- R=NO OF ENTRIES IN COL LESS 1.
250     R=M-1
260     L=0
270     A=-1
280     FOR K=1 TO N
290     R=R-1
300     A=-A
310     FOR I=0 TO M-K
320     D(I,K)=D(I+1,K-1)-D(I,K-1)
330     NEXT I
340     IF A<0 THEN 390
350     L=L+1
360     FOR I=0 TO R
370     C(I+L,L)=.5*(D(I+1,K)+D(I,K))
380     NEXT I
390     NEXT K
400     PRINT "X","Y","FORWARD DIFFERENCES UP TO ORDER";N
410     FOR I=0 TO M
420     PRINT X(I),Y(I),
430     FOR K=1 TO N-I
440     PRINT D(I,K),
450     NEXT K
460     PRINT
470     NEXT I
480     M1=INT(.1+.5*M)
490     PRINT "X","Y","MEAN CENTRAL DIFFCES, ODD ORDERS 1 TO";M1
500     FOR I=0 TO M1
510     PRINT X(I),Y(I),
520     FOR K=1 TO I
530     PRINT C(I,K),
540     NEXT K
550     PRINT
560     NEXT I
570     M2=INT(.6+.5*M)
580     L=M2-1
590     FOR I=M1+1 TO M
600     PRINT X(I),Y(I),
610     FOR K=1 TO L
620     PRINT C(I,K),
630     NEXT K
640     L=L-1
650     PRINT
660     NEXT I
670     END

Ready




RUN
THEDIF

NO OF DATA PTS LESS 1? 6
FIRST DATA POINT, X STEP? 0,.2
Y VALUES
?  0
? .198669
? .389418
? .564642
? .717356
? .841471
? .932039
NO OF COLUMNS OF DIFFERENCES? 6
X              Y              FORWARD DIFFERENCES UP TO ORDER 6
 0              0              .198669        -.00792         -.007605
.620008E-03    .275955E-03    -.308454E-04
.2             .198669        .190749        -.015525        -.698499E-02
.895962E-03    .245109E-03
.4             .389418        .175224        -.02251         -.608903E-02
.114107E-02
.6             .564642        .152714        -.028599        -.494796E-02

.8             .717356        .124115        -.033547
1              .841471        .090568
1.2            .932039
```

```
X               Y               MEAN CENTRAL DIFFCES, ODD ORDERS 1 TO 3
 0               0
.2              .198669         .194709
.4              .389418         .182987         -.007295
.6              .564642         .163969         -.653701E-02    .260532E-03

.8              .717356         .138415         -.55185E-02
1               .841471         .107341
1.2             .932039
Ready
```

Program notes

(1) In instructions 500 to 660, the odd order mean central differences are printed. In order to give a neat display, some tricky coding is involved! The number of columns of differences to be printed must increase from 1 to about $M/2$ and then decrease back to 1 as we progress down the rows. More precisely, if we define

$$M_1 = \begin{cases} M/2 & \text{for } M \text{ even} \\ (M-1)/2 & \text{for } M \text{ odd} \end{cases} \qquad M_2 = \begin{cases} M/2 & \text{for } M \text{ even} \\ (M+1)/2 & \text{for } M \text{ odd} \end{cases}$$

then there are from 1 to M_1 columns of entries for $I = 1$ to M_1, respectively, and from $M_2 - 1$ to 1 columns for $I = M_1 + 1$ to M, respectively.

(2) In each row of the tables, output is achieved by an instruction such as

530 PRINT C(I, K),

By following the PRINT with a comma, a row of entries is obtained. Clearly we would wish to continue neatly onto a new line if necessary. The way to achieve this may vary from one computer to another. In this program we use the VAX BASIC instruction

50 MARGIN 70

which specifies a page width of 70 characters, thus allowing space for precisely 5 prints (of 14 characters each). In the Sample Run a neat output is thus obtained in both the first two rows of forward differences, in spite of the fact that these over-run the line width by 3 and 2 entries, respectively.

5.4.3 *The shift operator and its relations to interpolation, differentiation and integration*

Let us now define operators C, D, and I which perform (exact) interpolation, differentiation, and indefinite integration, respectively, based on a data point (x_0, y_0). Specifically

$$\text{C}y_0 = y(x), \quad \text{D}y_0 = \left(\frac{dy}{dx}\right)_{x=x_0}, \quad \text{I}y_0 = \int_\alpha^{x_0} y(x)\,dx \quad (5.32)$$

where α is some fixed point. Here C stands for collocation, which is the technique used in interpolation. Links will now be established between each of these operators and the shift operator E.

Firstly, the problem of interpolation is that of determining a value of $y(x)$ at a point x, which is not an ordinate, in terms of known values at ordinates and specifically in terms of y_0. Thus y_p is required, where p is a given real number (but not an integer), from a series of values $y_0, \ldots, y_m$ at ordinates $x_0, \ldots, x_m$. Now from (5.21)

$$y(x) = y(x_p) = y_p = \text{E}^p y_0 \qquad (5.33)$$

where $x_p = x_0 + ph$. Hence we deduce from (5.32) and (5.33) that

$$\text{C} = \text{E}^p \qquad (5.34)$$

For the processes of differentiation and integration, the relations between D or I and E are more subtle. Clearly D and I are related by the equation

$$\text{I} = \text{D}^{-1} \qquad (5.35)$$

since integration is the inverse process to differentiation, and hence it suffices to relate D to E. This link is established by using a remarkable simplification of the infinite Taylor series expansion. Clearly

$$y(x_0 + h) = y(x_0) + hy_0' + \frac{h^2}{2!}y_0'' + \cdots + \frac{h^n}{n!}y_0^{(n)} + \cdots$$

If D^2 denotes (d^2/dx^2), etc, then it follows that

$$\text{E}y_0 = y_0 + h\text{D}y_0 + \frac{1}{2!}h^2\text{D}^2y_0 + \frac{1}{3!}h^3\text{D}^3y_0 + \cdots \frac{1}{n!}h^n\text{D}^ny_0 + \cdots$$

$$= \left[1 + (h\text{D}) + \frac{(h\text{D})^2}{2!} + \cdots + \frac{1}{n!}(h\text{D})^n + \cdots\right]y_0$$

$$= e^{h\text{D}}y_0$$

Hence

$$\text{E} = e^{h\text{D}} \qquad (5.36)$$

and the relation between E and D is established. We may also write

$$D = h^{-1} \log_e E \qquad (5.37)$$

and from (5.35) we may invert this relation to obtain

$$I = h(\log_e E)^{-1} \qquad (5.38)$$

5.5 Interpolation with equally spaced ordinates

To obtain an interpolation formula based on finite differences, it is now just a matter of combining the relation (5.34) between the operators C (interpolation) and E (shift) with the appropriate chosen relation among (5.22)–(5.26) between E and the various finite differences.

In the case of forward differences, (5.22), (5.33) and (5.34) give

$$y_p = Cy_0 = E^p y_0 = (1 + \Delta)^p y_0.$$

Using the binomial expansion,

$$y_p = \left[1 + \binom{p}{1}\Delta + \binom{p}{2}\Delta^2 + \cdots + \binom{p}{n}\Delta^n + \cdots \right] y_0 \quad (5.39)$$

where

$$\binom{p}{k} \equiv \frac{p(p-1)\ldots(p-k+1)}{1.2 \quad \ldots \quad k}$$

for all real p and integral k. Hence

$$y(x) = y(x_p) = y_p \simeq y_0 + \binom{p}{1}\Delta y + \binom{p}{2}\Delta^2 y_0 + \cdots + \binom{p}{n}\Delta^n y_0 \quad (5.40)$$

by truncating (5.39) at the term in Δ^n (for a chosen n). The approximation (5.40) to y_p (for p not an integer) is termed *Newton's forward difference interpolation formula*, and it has a truncation error of $O(h^{n+1})$, by (5.28), since the error is a series in powers of Δ starting with $\Delta^{n+1} y_0$. For example, for the data of Table 5.5, with $x = 1.05$, $h = .1$ and $p = .5$,

$$y(1.05) = y_{.5} \simeq 2.7183 + \frac{.5}{1}(.2859) + \frac{(.5)(-.5)}{1.2}(.0300)$$

$$+ \frac{(.5)(-.5)(-1.5)}{1 \cdot 2 \cdot 3}(.0033) + \frac{(.5)(-.5)(-1.5)(-2.5)}{1 \cdot 2 \cdot 3 \cdot 4}(.0001)$$

$$= 2.7183 + .1430 - .0038 + .0002 - .0000 = 2.8577$$

This result is correct to 4 decimal places, and the error is indeed behaving like $h^{N+1} = (.1)^5$.

Note that, for any k, $\begin{pmatrix} p \\ k \end{pmatrix}$ is a polynomial of degree k in p which is zero for $p = 0, 1, \ldots, k - 1$. It follows that $\begin{pmatrix} p \\ n + 1 \end{pmatrix}$, $\begin{pmatrix} p \\ n + 2 \end{pmatrix}$, $\ldots$ are all zero for p equal to $0, 1, \ldots, n$, and hence that the error in (5.40) is zero at these values. Thus (5.40) represents a polynomial of degree n in p which is exact for $p = 0, 1, \ldots, n$. The value of p for a given value of x is determined from

$$p = (x - x_0)/h \qquad (5.41)$$

where $x = x_p$. It follows that (5.40) represents the polynomial of degree n in x which collocates $y(x)$ at $x = x_0, x_1, \ldots, x_n$. In other words, Newton's interpolation formula (5.40) is achieved by polynomial collocation at $n + 1$ consecutive data points.

The following algorithm and program calculate $y(x)$ for a given x in a set of data with equally spaced ordinates:

Algorithm 5.4 Interpolation by Newton's forward difference formula

(i) Specify data (x_i, y_i) at an equal spacing of h in x, and calculate an array $\{d_{ik} = \Delta^k y_i\}$ of forward differences by Algorithm 5.3.
(ii) Specify x and hence determine p from (5.41).
(iii) Calculate $y(x)$ by (5.40) for a succession of values of n.

Program 5.4 NEWFOR: Newton's forward difference interpolation formula

```
LIST
NEWFOR

10      REM- NEWFOR: INTERPOLATES VALUES Y(X) AT SPECIFIED PTS
20      REM- IN A TABLE BY NEWTON FORWARD DIFFCE FORMULA (UP TO ORDER N)
30      DIM X(10),Y(10),D(10,10)
40      PRINT "NO OF DATA PTS LESS 1";
50      INPUT M
60      PRINT "FIRST DATA PT, X STEP";
70      INPUT X(0),H
80      FOR I=1 TO M
90      X(I)=X(I-1)+H
100     NEXT I
110     PRINT "Y VALUES"
120     FOR I=0 TO M
130     INPUT Y(I)
140     D(I,0)=Y(I)
150     NEXT I
160     PRINT "MAX ORDER OF NEWTON FORMULA";
170     INPUT N
180     REM- CALCULATES FORWARD DIFFERENCES
190     FOR K=1 TO N
200     FOR I=0 TO M-K
210     D(I,K)=D(I+1,K-1)-D(I,K-1)
220     NEXT I
230     NEXT K
240     PRINT "X VALUE FOR INTERPOLATION (TO STOP INPUT 1E11)";
250     INPUT Z
260     IF Z>1.E10 THEN 430
270     P=(Z-X(0))/H
280     PRINT "VALUE OF VARIABLE P:",P
```

```
290    REM- CALCULATES NEWTON FORMULA
300    E=Y(0)
310    U=P
320    V=1
330    W=1
340    PRINT "ORDER:","Y VALUE:"
350    FOR K=1 TO N
360    W=W*U/V
370    U=U-1
380    V=V+1
390    E=E+W*D(0,K)
400    PRINT K,E
410    NEXT K
420    GO TO 240
430    PRINT "END OF DATA"
440    END

Ready



RUN
NEWFOR

NO OF DATA PTS LESS 1? 4
FIRST DATA PT, X STEP? 1,.1
Y VALUES
? .841471
? .891207
? .932039
? .963558
? .98545
MAX ORDER OF NEWTON FORMULA? 4
X VALUE FOR INTERPOLATION (TO STOP INPUT 1E11)? 1.05
VALUE OF VARIABLE P:        .5
ORDER:      Y VALUE:
  1         .866339
  2         .867452
  3         .867426
  4         .867423
X VALUE FOR INTERPOLATION (TO STOP INPUT 1E11)? 1.35
VALUE OF VARIABLE P:        3.5
ORDER:      Y VALUE:
  1         1.01555
  2         .976592
  3         .975697
  4         .975723
X VALUE FOR INTERPOLATION (TO STOP INPUT 1E11)? 1E11
END OF DATA
Ready
```

A *Newton backward difference formula* may be obtained in a very similar way as follows.

$$y_p = Cy_0 = E^p y_0 = [(1 - \nabla)^{-1}]^p y_0 = (1 - \nabla)^{-p} y_0$$

$$= \left(1 + \binom{p}{1}\nabla + \binom{p+1}{2}\nabla^2 + \cdots \binom{p+n-1}{n}\nabla^n + \cdots\right)y_0$$

i.e.

$$y(x) = y_p \simeq y_0 + \binom{p}{1}\nabla y_0 + \binom{p+1}{2}\nabla^2 y_0 + \cdots + \binom{p+n-1}{n}\nabla^n y_0 \tag{5.42}$$

Here $x < x_0$, so that $p = (x - x_0)/h$ is negative, and again the truncation error is $O(h^{n+1})$.

For example, for the data of Table 5.6 with $x = 1.35$, $h = .1$,

$p = -.5$, and with x_i renumbered so that $x_0 = 1.4$, we obtain

$$y(1.35) = y_{3.5} \simeq 4.0552 + \frac{(-.5)}{1}(.3859) + \frac{(.5)(-.5)}{1 \cdot 2}(.0367)$$

$$+ \frac{(1.5)(.5)(-.5)}{1 \cdot 2 \cdot 3}(.0034) + \frac{(2.5)(1.5)(.5)(-.5)}{1 \cdot 2 \cdot 3 \cdot 4}(.0001)$$

$$= 4.0552 - .1930 - .0046 - .0002 - .0000 = 3.8574$$

Again the result is correct to 4 decimal places.

We shall not give an algorithm for (5.42). We simply remark that (5.42) is exactly equivalent to applying Newton's forward difference interpolation formula (5.40) to the table (x_i, y_i) after it has been displayed upside down (i.e. at a spacing of $-h$).

From the sample run of Program 5.4, we observe that although the formula (5.42) gives satisfactory answers throughout, it begins to lose accuracy as p increases. Indeed in central parts of a table it can sometimes be advantageous to adopt a formula based on central and mean central differences. For example one such formula, whose derivation is to be found in Henrici[2], is *Stirling's formula*

$$y(x) = y_p \simeq y_0 + p\mu\delta y_0 + \frac{p^2}{2!}\delta^2 y_0 + \binom{p+1}{3}\mu\delta^3 y_0 + \frac{p^2(p^2 - 1^2)}{4!}\delta^4 y_0$$

$$+ \binom{p+2}{5}\mu\delta^5 y_0 + \frac{p^2(p^2 - 1^2)(p^2 - 2^2)}{6!}\delta^6 y_0 + \cdots \quad (5.43)$$

We leave the application of this formula to the reader (Problem 8).

5.6 Differentiation

A *forward difference formula* for differentiation may be obtained by combining (5.22) and (5.37) as follows

$$Dy_0 = h^{-1} \log Ey_0 = h^{-1}\log(1 + \Delta)y_0$$

$$= h^{-1}\left(\Delta - \frac{\Delta^2}{2} + \frac{\Delta^3}{3} - \frac{\Delta^4}{4} + \cdots + (-1)^{n-1}\frac{\Delta^n}{n} + \cdots\right)y_0$$

i.e.

$$y_0' \simeq h^{-1}\left(\Delta y_0 - \tfrac{1}{2}\Delta^2 y_0 + \tfrac{1}{3}\Delta^3 y_0 - \cdots + \frac{(-1)^{n-1}}{n}\Delta^n y_0\right) \quad (5.44)$$

This formula calculates y_0' from the entries in *one row* of the forward difference table of the data (x_i, y_i), and clearly it is only to be recommended for use at the top of a table. It has a truncation error of $O(h^n)$, since the error $O(h^{n+1})$ of the bracketed term is multiplied by h^{-1}.

The corresponding *backward difference formula*, recommended only for use at the bottom of a table, is

$$\mathrm{D}y_0 = h^{-1}\log(1 - \nabla)^{-1}y_0 = h^{-1}\left(\nabla + \frac{\nabla^2}{2} + \frac{\nabla^3}{3} + \cdots\right)y_0$$

i.e.

$$y_0' \simeq h^{-1}\left(\nabla y_0 + \tfrac{1}{2}\nabla^2 y_0 + \tfrac{1}{3}\nabla^3 y_0 + \cdots + \frac{1}{n}\nabla^n y_0\right) \quad (5.45)$$

This formula is equivalent to applying the forward difference formula (5.44) to the function defined by the table of y in reverse order, using a negative step h.

At the centre of a table we use central and/or mean central differences, based on the formulae

$$E = e^{h\mathrm{D}} \quad \text{and} \quad 2\mu\delta = E - E^{-1},$$

from (5.36) and (5.26). Now

$$\mu\delta = \tfrac{1}{2}(e^{h\mathrm{D}} - e^{-h\mathrm{D}}) = \sinh h\mathrm{D}$$

and hence

$$y_0' = \mathrm{D}y_0 = h^{-1}\sinh^{-1}(\mu\delta)y_0 \quad (5.46)$$

By differentiating $\sinh^{-1} x$ at $x = 0$ and hence determining its Taylor series, we may deduce (see Problem 5) that

$$\sinh^{-1} x = x - \frac{1^2}{3!}x^3 + \frac{1^2 3^2}{5!}x^5 - \frac{1^2 3^2 5^2}{7!}x^7 + \cdots \quad (5.47)$$

and hence, by combining (5.46) and (5.47),

$$y_0' = h^{-1}\left(\mu\delta - \frac{1^2}{3!}\mu^3\delta^3 + \frac{1^2 3^2}{5!}\mu^5\delta^5 - \cdots\right)y_0$$

Now $\mu^2 = 1 + \tfrac{1}{4}\delta^2$ by (5.19), and so

$$y_0' = h^{-1}\left[\mu\delta - \tfrac{1}{6}\mu\left(1 + \frac{\delta^2}{4}\right)\delta^3 + \frac{3}{40}\mu\left(1 + \frac{\delta^2}{4}\right)^2\delta^5 - \cdots\right]y_0$$

Hence

$$y_0' = h^{-1}\left(\mu\delta y_0 - \tfrac{1}{6}\mu\delta^3 y_0 + \frac{1}{30}\mu\delta^5 y_0 - \frac{1}{140}\mu\delta^7 y_0 + \cdots\right) \quad (5.48)$$

Thus we have a formula based only on *mean central differences*.

As it stands, (5.48) is not suitable for use in a general BASIC program, since the coefficients are not expressed algebraically. However, by differentiating Stirling's formula (see Henrici[2]), such a general expression may be obtained in the form

$$y_0' \simeq h^{-1}\left\{\mu\delta y_0 - \frac{(1!)^2}{3!}\mu\delta^3 y_0 + \frac{(2!)^2}{5!}\mu\delta^5 y_0 - \cdots\right.$$

$$\left. + (-1)^{n-1}\frac{[(n-1)!]^2}{(2n-1)!}\mu\delta^{2n-1}y_0\right\} \quad (5.49)$$

Here the truncation error is $O(h^{2n-2})$, and so we note that only *about half* as many terms of (5.49) are required to obtain the same level of accuracy as in (5.44) or (5.45).

Using formulae (5.44), (5.45) and (5.48), respectively, for points at the top, bottom, and middle of Tables 5.5, 5.6, 5.7 we deduce that:

$$y'(1.0) = y_0'$$
$$\simeq (.1)^{-1}[.2859 - \tfrac{1}{2}(.0300) + \tfrac{1}{3}(.0033) - \tfrac{1}{4}(.0001) + \cdots]$$
$$= 10[.2589 - .0150 + .0011 - .0000] = 2.720$$

$$y'(1.4) = y_4'$$
$$\simeq (.1)^{-1}[.3859 + \tfrac{1}{2}(.0367) + \tfrac{1}{3}(.0034) + \tfrac{1}{4}(.0001) + \cdots]$$
$$= 10[.3859 + .0183 + .0011 + .0000] = 4.053$$

$$y'(1.2) = y_2'$$
$$\simeq (.1)^{-1}[.3326 - \tfrac{1}{6}(.0033) + \cdots] = 3.320$$

The correct gradients are 2.718, 4.055, and 3.320, respectively, and we observe that the mean central difference formula is indeed more accurate, although involving far less terms.

We now give a pair of programs for calculating derivatives; the first uses forward differences and formula (5.44), and the second uses mean central differences and formula (5.49). The relevant part of Program 5.3 is used to generate a difference table in each case.

Program 5.5 DIFFOR: Differentiation using forward differences

```
LIST
DIFFOR

10      REM- DIFFOR: CALCULATES DIFFERENTIAL Y'(X) AT GIVEN PTS X=Z
20      REM- IN A TABLE, USING A FORWARD DIFFERENCE FORMULA.
30      DIM X(10),Y(10),D(10,10)
40      PRINT "NO OF DATA PTS LESS 1";
50      INPUT M
60      PRINT "FIRST DATA POINT, X STEP";
70      INPUT X(0),H
80      FOR I=1 TO M
90      X(I)=X(I-1)+H
```

```
100      NEXT I
110      PRINT "Y VALUES"
120      FOR I=0 TO M
130      INPUT Y(I)
140      D(I,0)=Y(I)
150      NEXT I
160      PRINT "NO OF COLUMNS OF DIFFERENCES";
170      INPUT N
180      REM- CALCULATES FORWARD DIFFERENCES: K=COL, I=ROW
190      FOR K=1 TO N
200      FOR I=0 TO M-K
210      D(I,K)=D(I+1,K-1)-D(I,K-1)
220      NEXT I
230      NEXT K
240      PRINT "X VALUE (IN TABLE) FOR Y'(X) (TO STOP INPUT 1E11)";
250      INPUT Z
260      IF Z>1.E10 THEN 390
270      P=(Z-X(0))/H
280      PRINT "ORDINATE NUMBER P:",P
290      REM- CALCULATES FORMULA FOR Y'(X).
300      E=0
310      W=1/H
320      PRINT "ORDER:","Y VALUE:"
330      FOR K=1 TO N-P
340      E=E+W*D(P,K)/K
350      PRINT K,E
360      W=-W
370      NEXT K
380      GO TO 240
390      PRINT "END OF DATA"
400      END

Ready


RUN
DYFFOR

NO OF DATA PTS LESS 1? 4
FIRST DATA POINT, X STEP? 0,.2
Y VALUES
? 0
? .198669
? .389418
? .564642
? .717356
NO OF COLUMNS OF DIFFERENCES? 4
X VALUE (IN TABLE) FOR Y'(X) (TO STOP INPUT 1E11)? 0
ORDINATE NUMBER P:            0
ORDER:          Y VALUE:
  1               .993345
  2              1.01314
  3              1.00047
  4               .999695
X VALUE (IN TABLE) FOR Y'(X) (TO STOP INPUT 1E11)? .4
ORDINATE NUMBER P:            2
ORDER:          Y VALUE:
  1               .87612
  2               .932395
X VALUE (IN TABLE) FOR Y'(X) (TO STOP INPUT 1E11)? 1E11
END OF DATA
Ready
```

Program notes

(1) This program essentially follows Program 5.3 up to instruction 230.

(2) In the Sample Run, data of $y = \sin x$ are used. Note that at $x = 0$ (at the top of the table) it is clear that $y' = 1.000$ to 3 decimals. However, at $x = .4$ (in the centre of the table) there are just two results available which only agree in the first figure, and although we might hazard the value $y' = .93$ we would do so hesitatingly.

Program 5.6 DIFCEN: Differentiation using mean central differences

```
LIST
DIFCEN

10      REM- DIFCEN: CALCULATES DIFFERENTIAL Y'(X) AT GIVEN PTS X=Z
20      REM- IN A TABLE, USING A MEAN CENTRAL DIFFERENCE FORMULA.
30      REM- D(I,K),C(I,K) ARE FORWARD AND MEAN CENTRAL DIFFCES.
40      DIM X(10),Y(10),D(10,10),C(10,10)
50      PRINT "NO OF DATA PTS LESS 1";
60      INPUT M
70      PRINT "FIRST DATA POINT, X STEP";
80      INPUT X(0),H
90      FOR I=1 TO M
100     X(I)=X(I-1)+H
110     NEXT I
120     PRINT "Y VALUES"
130     FOR I=0 TO M
140     INPUT Y(I)
150     D(I,0)=Y(I)
160     C(I,0)=Y(I)
170     NEXT I
180     PRINT "NO OF COLUMNS OF DIFFERENCES";
190     INPUT N
200     REM- CALCULATES ODD ORDER MEAN CENTRAL DIFFERENCES:
210     R=M-1
220     L=0
230     A=-1
240     FOR K=1 TO N
250     R=R-1
260     A=-A
270     FOR I=0 TO M-K
280     D(I,K)=D(I+1,K-1)-D(I,K-1)
290     NEXT I
300     IF A<0 THEN 350
310     L=L+1
320     FOR I=0 TO R
330     C(I+L,L)=.5*(D(I+1,K)+D(I,K))
340     NEXT I
350     NEXT K
360     PRINT "X VALUE (IN TABLE) FOR Y'(X) (TO STOP INPUT 1E11)";
370     INPUT Z
380     IF Z>1.E10 THEN 610
390     P=(Z-X(0))/H
400     P=INT(P+.1)
410     PRINT "ORDINATE NUMBER P:";P
420     REM- CALCULATES Y'(X) BY MEAN CENTRAL DIFFCES.
430     E=0
440     W=1/H
450     PRINT "ORDER:","Y' VALUES:"
460     L=1
470     P1=P
480     IF M1>P THEN 500
490     P1=M-P
500     IF P1>0 THEN 530
510     PRINT "NO DIFFERENCES AVAILABLE"
520     GO TO 360
530     FOR K=1 TO P1
540     IF 0>J THEN 570
550     E=E+W*C(P,K)
560     PRINT L,E
570     W=-W*(K^2)/(2*K*(2*K+1))
580     L=L+2
590     NEXT K
600     GO TO 360
610     PRINT "END OF DATA"
620     END

Ready


RUN
DIFCEN

NO OF DATA PTS LESS 1? 6
FIRST DATA POINT, X STEP? .8,.1
Y VALUES
? .717356
? .783327
? .841471
? .891207
```

```
?  .932039
?  .963558
?  .98545
NO OF COLUMNS OF DIFFERENCES? 6
X VALUE (IN TABLE) FOR Y'(X) (TO STOP INPUT 1E11)? 1.1
ORDINATE NUMBER P: 3
ORDER:        Y' VALUES:
  1              .45284
  3              .453594
  5              .453596
X VALUE (IN TABLE) FOR Y'(X) (TO STOP INPUT )E11)? 1.2
ORDINATE NUMBER P: 4
ORDER:        Y' VALUES:
  1              .361755
  3              .362358
X VALUE (IN TABLE) FOR Y'(X) (TO STOP INPUT 1E11)? 1E11
END OF DATA
Ready
```

Program notes

(1) This program essentially follows Program 5.3 up to instruction 350.

(2) Results for y' at the centre of the table are clearly very satisfactory. Although only 2 results are available at $x = 1.2$, these agree to 3 decimals, and this demonstrates the rapid convergence of the central difference method.

5.7 Integration

Both forward differences and central differences may be used to integrate functions, by making use of the relation (5.38) between I and E. Firstly, from (5.32), the integral I_{01} of $y(x)$ from x_0 to x_1 may be expressed as

$$I_{01} = \int_{x_0}^{x_1} y(x)\, dx = \int_{\alpha}^{x_1} y(x)\, dx - \int_{\alpha}^{x_0} y(x)\, dx = Iy_1 - Iy_0 = I(y_1 - y_0)$$

In Figure 5.1, this represents the area under the graph $y = y(x)$ between $x = x_0$ and $x = x_1$. Thus

$$I_{01} = \int_{x_0}^{x_1} y(x)\, dx = I\Delta y_0 \qquad (5.50)$$

Hence, by (5.38),

$$I_{01} = h(\log E)^{-1}\Delta y_0 \qquad (5.51)$$

Now, expressing E in terms of forward differences using (5.22),

$$I_{01} = h\{\log(1 + \Delta)\}^{-1}\Delta y_0$$

$$= h\left\{\Delta - \frac{\Delta^2}{2} + \frac{\Delta^3}{3} - \cdots\right\}^{-1}\Delta y_0 = h\Delta^{-1}\left\{1 - \frac{\Delta}{2} + \frac{\Delta^2}{3} - \cdots\right\}^{-1}\Delta y_0$$

$$= h\left\{1 + \left(-\frac{\Delta}{2} + \frac{\Delta^2}{3} - \cdots\right)\right\}^{-1} y_0 = h\left\{1 - \left(-\frac{\Delta}{2} + \frac{\Delta^2}{3} - \cdots\right)\right.$$

$$+ \left(-\frac{\Delta}{2} + \frac{\Delta^2}{3} - \cdots\right)^2 - \cdots\left.\right\} y_0 \tag{5.52}$$

[Here we use the expression: $(1 + t)^{-1} = 1 - t + t^2 - t^3 + \cdots$.]
From (5.28) we deduce that, to an accuracy of $O(h^3)$,

$$I_{01} \simeq h\left(1 + \frac{\Delta}{2}\right) y = h[y_0 + \tfrac{1}{2}(y_1 - y_0)] = \frac{h}{2}(y_0 + y_1)$$

Thus

$$\int_{x_0}^{x_1} y(x)\,dx \simeq \frac{h}{2}(y_0 + y_1) \tag{5.53}$$

with truncation error $O(h^3)$.

This is called the *trapezium rule* for integration and is equivalent, in Figure 5.1, to replacing the curve P_0P_1 by a straight line.

If we require an integral from $x = a$ to $x = b$, then the interval $[a, b]$ is split into, say, n subintervals $[x_0, x_1], [x_1, x_2], \ldots, [x_{n-1}, x_n]$, where $x_0 = a$ and $x_n = b$. Each subinterval is of equal length h, so that

$$h = \frac{b - a}{n} \quad \text{and} \quad x_i = x_0 + ih \qquad (i = 0, 1, \ldots, n)$$

Clearly this is consistent with the current notation for data (x_i, y_i). Then, by applying (5.53) in each subinterval, we obtain the *extended trapezium rule*

$$\int_a^b y(x)\,dx = \int_{x_0}^{x_1} + \int_{x_1}^{x_2} + \cdots + \int_{x_{n-1}}^{x_n} y(x)\,dx$$

$$\simeq \frac{h}{2}[(y_0 + y_1) + (y_1 + y_2) + \cdots + (y_{n-1} + y_n)]$$

i.e.

$$\int_a^b y(x)\,dx \simeq T_n = h[\tfrac{1}{2}(y_0 + y_n) + (y_1 + y_2 + \cdots + y_{n-1})] \tag{5.54}$$

with error $O(h^2)$.

The notation T_n is used here to denote the 'extended trapezoidal rule with n steps'. Since the truncation error in (5.54) contains n contributions each of $O(h^3)$, where n is proportional to h^{-1}, the accumulated error is clearly $O(h^2)$.

A program which calculates (5.54) is given below. For simplicity $y = y(x)$ is defined as a function throughout $[a, b]$, though the program may be modified to cope with tabulated data.

Program 5.7 TRAP: Trapezium rule

```
LIST
TRAP

10   REM- TRAP: INTEGRATES Y=Y(X) FROM X=A TO X=B
20   REM- USES TRAPEZIUM RULE WITH N STEPS
30   REM- THE INTEGRAND IS SPECIFIED BY THE DEFINED FUNCTION FNY(X)
40   PRINT "LIMITS OF INTEGRATION A,B";
50   INPUT A,B
60   PRINT "NO OF STEPS";
70   INPUT N
80   IF N=0 THEN 190
90   H=(B-A)/N
100  T=.5*(FNY(A)+FNY(B))
110  X=A
120  FOR I=1 TO N-1
130  X=X+H
140  T=T+FNY(X)
150  NEXT I
160  T=H*T
170  PRINT "TRAPEZIUM SUM : ",T
180  GO TO 60
190  PRINT"NO MORE DATA"
200  DEF FNY(X)=EXP(-.5*X*X)/SQRT(2*PI)
250  END

Ready


RUN
TRAP

LIMITS OF INTEGRATION A,B? 0,5
NO OF STEPS? 2
TRAPEZIUM SUM :              .5425
NO OF STEPS? 4
TRAPEZIUM SUM :              .500002
NO OF STEPS? 8
TRAPEZIUM SUM :              .5
NO OF STEPS? 0
NO MORE DATA
Ready


200 DEF FNY(X)=TAN(X)
RUN
TRAP

LIMITS OF INTEGRATION A,B? 0,1.0472
NO OF STEPS? 8
TRAPEZIUM SUM :              .697404
NO OF STEPS? 16
TRAPEZIUM SUM :              .694221
NO OF STEPS? 32
TRAPEZIUM SUM :              .693419
NO OF STEPS? 64
TRAPEZIUM SUM :              .693218
NO OF STEPS? 128
TRAPEZIUM SUM :              .693169
NO OF STEPS? 0
NO MORE DATA
Ready
```

Program notes

(1) For ease of programming, indices 0, 1, . . . , n have not been used at all to implement (5.54). Instead we have simply observed that $y_0 = y(a)$ and $y_n = y(b)$, and the values x_i, $y(x_i)$ have been calculated as $x, y(x)$ for all $i = 1, . . . , n - 1$, where x is increased by h for each new i.

(2) In Sample Run 1, the program calculates

$$\frac{1}{\sqrt{2\pi}} \int_0^{\infty} \exp(-\tfrac{1}{2}x^2)\, dx$$

by replacing ∞ by 5. This integral is the area under the positive half of the 'normal distribution' curve.

(3) In Sample Run 2, a new function $y = \tan x$ is defined, and its integral from 0 to $\pi/3$ is calculated. Why is the answer log 2?

5.7.1 *Simpson's rule*

If the interval $[a, b]$ is split up into an *even* number n of divisions, then the area under $y = y(x)$ may be calculated by adding the areas from x_0 to x_2, x_2 to $x_4, . . . , x_{n-2}$ to x_n, and using an integration rule based on sets of three points $[P_0, P_1\ P_2]$; $[P_2, P_3, P_4]$; . . . corresponding to two steps of h at a time. Indeed if a parabola is drawn through P_0, P_1, P_2, and the area under this curve is calculated (to approximate that under $y = y(x)$) then it is not difficult to show (Problem 11) that we obtain *Simpson's rule*.

$$\int_{x_0}^{x_2} y(x)\, dx \simeq \frac{h}{3}\,(y_0 + 4y_1 + y_2)$$

In fact this formula may be obtained by using central differences in place of forward differences, as follows

$$\int_{x_0}^{x_2} y(x)\, dx = \mathrm{I}y_2 - \mathrm{I}y_0 = \mathrm{I}(2\mu\delta y_1) \quad \text{from (5.15)}$$

$$= h(h\mathrm{D})^{-1}2\mu\delta y_1 = h[\sinh^{-1}(\mu\delta)]^{-1}2\mu\delta y_1 \quad \text{from (5.46)}$$

$$= h[\mu\delta - \tfrac{1}{6}\mu^3\delta^3 + O(h^5)]^{-1}2\mu\delta y_1 \quad \text{from (5.47) and} \quad (5.28)$$

$$= 2h[1 - \tfrac{1}{6}\mu^2\delta^2 + O(h^4)]^{-1}y_1 \quad \text{where} \quad \mu^2 = 1 + \tfrac{1}{4}\delta^2 \quad \text{from (5.19)}$$

$$= 2h[1 - \tfrac{1}{6}\delta^2 + O(h^4)]^{-1}y_1 = 2h[y_1 + \tfrac{1}{6}\delta^2 y_1] + O(h^5)$$

$$= 2h[y_1 + \tfrac{1}{6}(y_2 - 2y_1 + y_0)] + O(h^5)$$

Hence

$$\int_{x_0}^{x_2} y(x)\,dx \approx \frac{h}{3}(y_0 + 4y_1 + y_2) \text{ with truncation error } O(h^5) \quad (5.55)$$

By applying this formula successively for $n/2$ steps of $2h$ to calculate integrals over $[x_0, x_2], [x_2, x_4], \ldots, [x_{n-2}, x_n]$, we obtain the *extended Simpson's rule*

$$I^* = \int_a^b y(x)\,dx \approx S_n = \frac{h}{3} \sum_{i=0}^{n-2} (y_i + 4y_{i+1} + y_{i+2})$$

summed over even i

$$= \frac{h}{3}[y_0 + y_n + 4(y_1 + y_3 + \cdots + y_{n-1}) + 2(y_2 + y_4 + \cdots + y_{n-2})]$$
$$(5.56)$$

where $x_0 = a, x_n = b, h = (b - a)/n$, and n is even. The truncation error in this formula, obtained by accumulating $n/2$ errors of $O(h^5)$, where $n \propto h^{-1}$, is thus $O(h^4)$.

More generally, we may only wish to use part of the data. Suppose that every pth point is used in a total of m divisions of $[a, b]$, so that $n = mp$. Then

$$I^* \approx S_m = \frac{h}{3}[y_0 + y_{mp} + 4(y_p + y_{3p} + \cdots + y_{(m-1)p})$$
$$+ 2(y_{2p} + y_{4p} + \cdots + y_{(m-2)p})] \quad (5.57)$$

where now $h = (b - a)/m$ and $mp = n$. For example, consider the data in Table 5.10 which is in fact taken from the function $y = \log_e x$. For $m = 2, p = 2$,

$$S_2 = \frac{2.0}{3}(y_0 + 4y_2 + y_4) = 4.003$$

For $m = 4, p = 1$,

$$S_4 = \frac{1.0}{3}[(y_0 + 4y_1 + y_2) + (y_2 + 4y_3 + y_4)]$$

$$= \frac{1.0}{3}[y_0 + y_4 + 4(y_1 + y_3) + 2y_2] = 4.041$$

The true solution is

$$\int_1^5 \log x\,dx = 5\log 5 - 4 = 4.047.$$

Here only every second point needs to be used for 1% accuracy.

The following program performs Simpson's rule to integrate a function defined throughout an interval, and it is tested for $y = \cos x$ and $[a, b] = [0, \pi/2]$. No program will be given for a function defined on a discrete data set, but this is left as an exercise to the reader (Problem 13).

Table 5.10 Discrete data of $\log_e x$

i	0	1	2	3	4
x_i	1.0	2.0	3.0	4.0	5.0
y_i	0	0.693	1.099	1.386	1.609

Program 5.8 SIMPSN: Simpson's rule

```
LIST
SIMPSN

10   REM- SIMPSN: CALCULATES INTEGRAL OF Y=Y(X) FROM X=A TO X=B.
20   REM- USES SIMPSON'S RULE WITH 2,4,8,...,2**P STATIONS
30   PRINT "INTERVAL END POINTS A,B ";
40   INPUT A,B
50   PRINT "VALUE P (<11) FOR 2**P STATIONS ";
60   INPUT P
70   PRINT "NO OF PTS  ,    SIMPSON SUM"
80   N=2
90   M=1
100  FOR K=1 TO P
110  X=A
120  H=(B-A)/N
130  S=0
140  FOR I=0 TO M-1
150  S=S+H*(FNY(X)+4*FNY(X+H)+FNY(X+2*H))/3
160  X=X+2*H
170  NEXT I
180  PRINT N,S
190  N=2*N
200  M=2*M
210  NEXT K
220  REM- FNY(X) IS INTEGRAND TO BE DEFINED HERE
230  DEF FNY(X)=COS(X)
240  END

Ready
```

```
RUN
SIMPSN

INTERVAL END POINTS A,B ? 0,1.570796
VALUE P (<11) FOR 2**P STATIONS ? 4
NO OF PTS  ,    SIMPSON SUM
 2          1.00228
 4          1.00013
 8          1.00001
 16         1
Ready
```

Program notes

(1) As in Program 5.7, the index i has been dispensed with. The values x_i, x_{i+1}, x_{i+2} have been replaced by $x, x + h, x + 2h$, with x updated by $2h$ for each new i.

5.7.2 *Romberg Integration*

Knowledge of the nature of the truncation error in the trapezium rule may be exploited to obtain new and better algorithms. A more specific form of the error in the trapezium rule (5.54) may be shown to be

$$I^* = T_n + c_1 h^2 + c_2 h^4 + c_3 h^6 + \cdots$$

for some $c_1, c_2, \ldots$. If the number of subdivisions is doubled, then it follows that, if $y(x)$ is a 'sufficiently smooth' function,

$$I^* = T_{2n} + c_1(h/2)^2 + c_2(h/2)^4 + c_3(h/2)^6 + \cdots$$

If we subtract the first equation from four times the second, we eliminate the term in h^2 and obtain

$$3I^* = (4T_{2n} - T_n) - c_2 \tfrac{3}{4} h^4 - c_3 \tfrac{15}{16} h^6 - \cdots$$

Hence, $I^* \simeq (4T_{2n} - T_n)/3$ with error $O(h^4)$. Thus, by combining two trapezium results of $O(h^2)$ accuracy, we have obtained a new result of $O(h^4)$ accuracy. In fact the formula $(4T_{2n} - T_n)/3$ is easily seen to be identical to Simpson's rule (Problem 12).

The above process can be repeated. If we write

$$T_n^{(0)} = T_n, \quad T_n^{(1)} = S_{2n} = (4T_{2n}^{(0)} - T_n^{(0)})/3$$

then in a similar way we may combine two results $T_n^{(1)}$ and $T_{2n}^{(1)}$ to eliminate the error term in h^4:

$$I^* \simeq \frac{4^2 T_{2n}^{(1)} - T_n^{(1)}}{4^2 - 1} = \frac{16 T_{2n}^{(1)} - T_n^{(1)}}{15}$$

with error $O(h^6)$. This process may be repeated indefinitely, and the general formula, which is termed *Romberg integration*, takes the form

$$I^* \simeq T_n^{(k)} = \frac{4^k T_{2n}^{(k-1)} - T_n^{(k-1)}}{4^k - 1} \qquad (k = 1, 2, 3, \ldots) \quad (5.58)$$

with error $O(h^{2k+2})$.

This method is, however, only valid as long as $y(x)$ can be differentiated to an appropriately high degree. Furthermore it is strictly speaking only applicable for n 'sufficiently large'. This means that, if the trapezium rule results include a small value like $n = 1$ or 2, then the sequence $T_n^{(1)}, T_n^{(2)}, T_n^{(3)}, \ldots$ may not improve with each cycle.

The algorithm and program below implement Romberg integration, and Simpson's rule is automatically included as the first cycle of the Romberg scheme. The integrand $y = y(x)$ is specified as a defined function.

Algorithm 5.9 Romberg integration (including trapezium and Simpson rules)

(i) Define the interval $[a, b]$ and spacing h, define $y = y(x)$, and specify the number p of Romberg cycles.

(ii) Calculate a sequence $\{T_n^{(0)}\}$ of extended trapezium rule results for $n = 2, 4, 8, \ldots, 2^{p+1}$ from (5.54).

(iii) Calculate the array $\{T_n^{(k)}\}$ of Romberg results from (5.58) for $k = 1, 2, \ldots, p$ and $n = 2, 4, \ldots, 2^{p-k+1}$. The value $T_2^{(p)}$ is assumed to give the most accurate integral.

Program 5.9 ROMBG: Romberg integration

```
LIST
ROMBG

10   REM- ROMBG:  INTEGRATES Y=Y(X) FROM X=A TO X=B
20   REM-   USES TRAPEZIUM RULE WITH 2,4,8,...,2^P STEPS (P<11)
30   REM-   THEN USES ROMBERG SCHEME TO EXTEND ACCURACY
40   DIMENSION Z(10)
50   PRINT "INTERVAL END PTS A,B";
60   INPUT A,B
70   PRINT "MAX NO OF STEPS: 2 TO THE POWER";
80   INPUT P
90   PRINT "NO OF ROMBERG CYCLES";
100  INPUT R
110  PRINT "NO OF STEPS:","TRAPEZIUM SUM:"
120  N=2
130  REM- CALCULATES TRAP RULE APPROXN Z(I)
140  REM- BASED ON 2^I STEPS (I=1 TO P)
150  H=(B-A)/N
160  FOR I=1 TO P
170  X=A
180  T=.5*(FNY(A)+FNY(B))
190  FOR K=1 TO N-1
200  X=X+H
210  T=T+FNY(X)
220  NEXT K
230  Z(I)=H*T
240  PRINT N,Z(I)
250  N=2*N
260  H=.5*H
270  NEXT I
280  REM- USES ROMBERG SCHEME R TIMES (CYCLE 1 IS SIMPSON RULE)
290  REM-   ROMBERG CYCLES 1,...,R GIVE P-1,...,P-R RESULTS
300  C=4
310  N=2
320  FOR I=1 TO R
330  PRINT " ROMBERG CYCLE :",I
340  PRINT "VALUE OF N:","ROMBERG RESULT:"
350  N1=N
360  K=P-I
370  IF 1 > K THEN 460
380  FOR J=1 TO K
390  Z(J)=(C*Z(J+1)-Z(J))/(C-1)
400  PRINT N1,Z(J)
410  N1=2*N1
```

```
420 NEXT J
430 C=4*C
440 NEXT I
450 GO TO 470
460 PRINT " NO MORE CYCLES POSSIBLE"
470 REM-   FNY(X) IS THE INTEGRAND Y(X)
480 DEF FNY(X)=TAN(X)
490 END

Ready


RUN
ROMBG

INTERVAL END PTS A,B? 0,1.0472
MAX NO OF STEPS: 2 TO THE POWER? 3
NO OF ROMBERG CYCLES? 2
NO OF STEPS:   TRAPEZIUM SUM:
 2             .755755
 4             .709828
 8             .697404
 ROMBERG CYCLE :               1
VALUE OF N:    ROMBERG RESULT:
 2             .694519
 4             .693263
 ROMBERG CYCLE :               2
VALUE OF N:    ROMBERG RESULT:
 2             .693179
Ready
```

Program notes

(1) To save space, a single array $Z(1), \ldots, Z(P)$ is used to store $T_n^{(k)}$ for $n = 2, 4, \ldots, 2^p$ (for every k). (Initially $Z(1), \ldots, Z(P)$ are the trapezium sums for these values of n.) Thus, if $T_n^{(k)}$ is stored as $Z(J)$, then $T_{2n}^{(k)}$ will be stored as $Z(J + 1)$, and so we see the correspondence between instruction 390 in the program and Equation (5.58), with $C = 4^k$.

5.7.3 One step integration of high accuracy

Simpson's rule of Section 5.7.1 above, which is of relatively high accuracy, is based on integrating over two steps of h at a time, such as from x_0 to x_2. However we sometimes wish to calculate the integral I_{01} from x_0 to x_1 in just *one step*, especially if no data is available in between. In that case, formulae of high accuracy may be obtained from the expansion

$$I_{01} = h\left(y_0 + \tfrac{1}{2}\Delta y_0 - \frac{1}{12}\Delta^2 y_0 + \frac{1}{24}\Delta^3 y_0 - \frac{19}{720}\Delta^4 y_0 + \cdots\right) \quad (5.59)$$

which follows from (5.52) (Problem 15). In particular, stopping at $\Delta^2 y_0$,

$$I_{01} = h\left[y_0 + \tfrac{1}{2}(y_1 - y_0) - \frac{1}{12}(y_2 - 2y_1 + y_0)\right] + O(h^4)$$

i.e.

$$I_{01} \simeq \frac{h}{12}(5y_0 + 8y_1 - y_2) \quad \text{with truncation error } O(h^4). \quad (5.60)$$

This error is of the same order as the error in Simpson's rule.
For example, applying (5.59) to the data of Table 5.5 ($y = e^x$),

$$I_{01} = \int_{1.0}^{1.1} y \, dx = .1[2.7183 + \tfrac{1}{2}(.2859) - \tfrac{1}{12}(.0300) + \tfrac{1}{24}(.0033) -$$
$$= .1[2.7183 + .1430 - .0025 + .0001 - \ldots]$$
$$= 0.2859$$

This result is correct to 4 figures, and we only require the first
three terms, namely (5.60).

5.8 Indefinite integration

Suppose that we are given discrete data (x_i, y_i), where $y_i = y(x_i)$
and h is the step in x, and that we wish to tabulate at $\{x_i\}$ the
integrated or second integrated functions $z(x)$ and $w(x)$, that is

$$z(x) = z(x_0) + \int_{x_0}^{x} y(x) \, dx$$

and
$$\left. \vphantom{\int} \right\} \quad (5.61)$$

$$w(x) = w(x_0) + \int_{x_0}^{x} z(x) \, dx$$

For example, we may be given data of acceleration against time
and wish to tabulate the resulting velocity and displacement at
each time interval. The resulting data may be named as

$$z_i = z(x_i), \quad w_i = w(x_i) \qquad i = 0, 1, \ldots, n \qquad (5.62)$$

and clearly z_0 and w_0 need to be specified.

If not too much accuracy is required, then the trapezium rule
could be used to calculate z_i and w_i $(i = 1, \ldots, n)$ successively
from the formulae

$$z_i = z_{i-1} + \frac{h}{2}(y_{i-1} + y_i), \quad w_i = w_{i-1} + \frac{h}{2}(z_{i-1} + z_i) \qquad (i = 1, 2, \ldots)$$
$$(5.63)$$

with truncation errors of $O(h^2)$. The programming of such a simple algorithm is left as an exercise to the reader (Problem 16).

However, since greater accuracy is typically required, we now give a program for indefinite integration based on two $O(h^4)$ rules; the forward difference rule (5.60) for the first step, and Simpson's rule thereafter.

Algorithm 5.10 Repeated indefinite integration by a modified Simpson's rule

(i) Specify x_0, the spacing h, the first three abscissae y_0, y_1, y_2, and the initial values z_0, w_0.

(ii) Define

$$z_1 = z_0 + \frac{h}{12}(5y_0 + 8y_1 - y_2), \quad z_2 = z_0 + \frac{h}{3}(y_0 + 4y_1 + y_2)$$

$$w_1 = w_0 + \frac{h}{12}(5z_0 + 8z_1 - z_2), \quad w_2 = w_0 + \frac{h}{3}(z_0 + 4z_1 + z_2)$$

(iii) For $i = 3, 4, \ldots$, specify y_i (for $i > 2$), and define

$$z_i = z_{i-2} + \frac{h}{3}(y_{i-2} + 4y_{i-1} + y_i), \quad w_i = w_{i-2} + \frac{h}{3}(z_{i-2} + 4z_{i-1} + z_i)$$

These are the required values of the integrated and twice integrated data.

Program 5.10 SIMSIM: Repeated indefinite integration

```
LIST
SIMSIM

10      REM- SIMSIM: OBTAINS FIRST (INDEFINITE) INTEGRAL Z(X) AND
20      REM- SECOND INTEGRAL W(X) OF GIVEN FUNCTION Y(X),
30      REM- BY A MODIFIED SIMPSON'S RULE REPEATED.
40      DIM X(100),Y(100),Z(100),W(100)
50      PRINT "END POINTS A,B";
60      INPUT X(0),B
70      PRINT "SPACING H";
80      INPUT H
90      PRINT "INITIAL Z AND W";
100     INPUT Z(0),W(0)
110     PRINT "FIRST 3 Y VALUES"
120     INPUT Y(0),Y(1),Y(2)
130     N=INT(.1+(B-X(0))/H)
140     REM- CALCULATES FIRST TWO Z AND W VALUES
150     Z(1)=Z(0)+H*(5*Y(0)+8*Y(1)-Y(2))/12
160     Z(2)=Z(0)+H*(Y(0)+4*Y(1)+Y(2))/3
170     W(1)=W(0)+H*(5*Z(0)+8*Z(1)-Z(2))/12
180     W(2)=W(0)+H*(Z(0)+4*Z(1)+Z(2))/3
190     X(1)=X(0)+H
200     X(2)=X(1)+H
210     FOR I=0 TO 2
220     PRINT "X:";X(I);"Y:";Y(I);"Z:";Z(I);"W:";W(I)
230     NEXT I
240     REM- CALCULATES Z AND W VALUES STEP-BY-STEP
250     FOR I=3 TO N
260     PRINT "NEXT Y";
270     INPUT Y(I)
```

```
280    Z(I)=Z(I-2)+H*(Y(I-2)+4*Y(I-1)+Y(I))/3
290    W(I)=W(I-2)+H*(Z(I-2)+4*Z(I-1)+Z(I))/3
300    X(I)=X(I-1)+H
310    PRINT "X:";X(I);"Y:";Y(I);"Z:";Z(I);"W:";W(I)
320    NEXT I
330    END

Ready




RUN
SIMSIM

END POINTS A,B? 1,1.4
SPACING H? .1
INITIAL Z AND W? 2.7183,2.7183
FIRST 3 Y VALUES
? 2.7183
? 3.0042
? 3.3201
X: 1 Y: 2.7183 Z: 2.7183 W: 2.7183
X: 1.1 Y: 3.0042 Z: 3.00418 W: 3.00417
X: 1.2 Y: 3.3201 Z: 3.32014 W: 3.32014
NEXT Y? 3.6693
X: 1.3 Y: 3.6693 Z: 3.66931 W: 3.66931
NEXT Y? 4.0552
X: 1.4 Y: 4.0552 Z: 4.05522 W: 4.05522
Ready




RUN
SIMSIM

END POINTS A,B? 0,.4
SPACING H? .1
INITIAL Z AND W? -1,0
FIRST 3 Y VALUES
? 0
? .0998334
? .198669
X: 0 Y: 0 Z:-1 W: 0
X: .1 Y: .998334E-01 Z:-.995 W:-.998328E-01
X: .2 Y: .198669 Z:-.980067 W:-.198669
NEXT Y? .29552
X: .3 Y: .29552 Z:-.955332 W:-.295519
NEXT Y? .389418
X: .4 Y: .389418 Z:-.921061 W:-.389417
Ready
```

Program notes

(1) In Sample Run 1, data of $y(x) = e^x$ are integrated twice, starting at $x = 1$ with $z(1) = w(1) = e$. Clearly the solutions $z(x) = w(x) = e^x$ are obtained accurately at the data ordinates.

(2) In Sample Run 2, data of $y(x) = \sin x$ are integrated, starting at $x = 0$ with $z(0) = -1$, $w(0) = 0$. Clearly the solutions $z(x) = -\cos x$, $w(x) = -\sin x$ are obtained accurately at the data ordinates.

5.9 References

1. J.C. Mason, *BASIC Matrix Methods*, Butterworths, (1984)
2. P. Henrici, *Elements of Numerical Analysis*, Wiley, London, (1964)

PROBLEMS

(5.1) The data below correspond to $y = \sin x$. By reversing the variables and taking the data to correspond to $x = \sin^{-1} y$, use the Lagrange interpolation formula (Program 5.1) to calculate $\sin^{-1} y$ for $y = .7, .8, .9, 1$. Such a process of finding the value of x at which y takes a given value is termed *inverse interpolation*.

x	0.8	0.9	1.0	1.1	1.2	1.3	1.4
y	0.7174	0.7833	0.8415	0.8912	0.9320	0.9636	0.9855

(5.2) Use Neville's algorithm (Program 5.2) with $m = 3$ to interpolate at $x = 1.1$ in the following data

i	x_i	y_i
1	1.0	2.7183
2	1.2	3.3201
3	1.4	4.0552

Test the correctness of the program, by calculating P_{21}, P_{31}, and P_{32} by hand from (5.9). P_{21}, P_{31} are the straight lines which collocate the data x_1, x_2 and x_2, x_3, respectively.

(5.3) Prove by induction the validity of the recurrence (5.9) which defines Neville's algorithm. Hint: Assume that columns $r = 0, 1, \ldots, q - 1$ of Figure 5.1 have been defined correctly by (5.9), so that P_{ir} collocates at $x_{i-r}, \ldots, x_i$ for $i = 1, \ldots, m$; $r = 0, 1, \ldots, q - 1$. Deduce that, if P_{iq} is defined by (5.9), then it collocates at $x_{i-q}, \ldots, x_i$.

(5.4) Use Program 5.3 to calculate forward and mean central difference tables for the data

x	1.0	1.1	1.2	1.3	1.4
y	2.7183	3.0042	3.3201	3.6693	4.0552

Verify that the entries in Tables 5.5 to 5.7 are reproduced.

(5.5) Determine the Maclaurin series (at $x = 0$) of the function $y = \sinh^{-1} x$ in the form (5.47) (by calculating $y(0), y'(0), y''(0), \ldots$).

(5.6) Calculate $y(1.1), y'(1.0), y'(3.0)$ as accurately as you can for the data below

x	1.0	2.0	3.0	4.0	5.0
y	0	0.13863	0.32958	0.55452	0.80472

(5.7) Use Newton's *backward* difference interpolation formula to calculate $y(1.35)$ for the data of Problem 4. Hint: Write the data in

the reverse order, with $x_0 = 1.4$ and $h = -0.1$, and then use Newton's forward formula, as in Program 5.4.

(5.8) Prove that, if Stirling's formula (5.43) is truncated after its
term in $\delta^4 y_0$, then the resulting formula is exact at $x = x_{-2}, x_{-1}, x_0,$
x_1, x_2. Use this particular formula to interpolate $y(1.25)$ for the
data of Problem 4, with $x_0 = 1.2$ and $h = .1$.

(5.9) A table is given below, which records distance against time
for a certain car accelerating from rest. Use Programs 5.5 and 5.6
to calculate the velocity initially and after 5 seconds. How long
does the car take to travel 300 feet?

Time (sec)	0	1	2	3	4	5	6	7	8	9	10
Dist (ft)	0	14	41	76	117	163	215	271	331	395	463

(5.10) By noting that

$$D^2 = h^{-2}(\Delta - \tfrac{1}{2}\Delta^2 + \tfrac{1}{3}\Delta^3 - \cdots)^2 y_i \qquad \text{from (5.44)}$$

$$= h^{-2}(\mu\delta - \tfrac{1}{6}\mu\delta^3 + \tfrac{1}{30}\mu\delta^5 - \cdots)^2 y_i \qquad \text{from (5.45)}$$

$$= h^{-2}(\nabla + \tfrac{1}{2}\nabla^2 + \tfrac{1}{3}\nabla^3 + \cdots)^2 y_i \qquad \text{from (5.48)}$$

deduce that

$$y_i'' = h^{-2}(\Delta^2 - \Delta^3 + \tfrac{11}{12}\Delta^4 + \cdots)y_i = h^{-2}(\delta^2 - \tfrac{1}{12}\delta^4 + \tfrac{1}{90}\delta^6 + \cdots)y_i$$

$$= h^{-2}(\nabla^2 + \nabla^3 + \tfrac{11}{12}\nabla^4 + \cdots)y_i$$

Hence calculate $y''(x)$ at $x = 1.0, 1.2, 1.4$ for the data of Problem
4.

(5.11) Suppose that (x_{-1}, y_{-1}), (x_0, y_0), (x_1, y_1) are three data
points, equally spaced by h in x with $x_0 = 0$, (so that $x_{-1} = -h$,
$x_1 = h$). By applying the Lagrange interpolation formula, show
that

$$y = p(x) = (2h^2)^{-1}[(x^2 - xh)y_{-1} - 2(x^2 - h^2)y_0 + (x^2 + xh)y_1]$$

is the parabola which collocates $y = y(x)$ in the three data points.
Deduce that

$$\int_{x_{-1}}^{x_1} p(x)\, dx = \frac{h}{3}(y_{-1} + 4y_0 + y_1)$$

and hence that Simpson's rule is obtained by integrating a parabola
which collocates in three data points.

(5.12) Show that the first cycle of Romberg integration is
Simpson's rule. Hint:

$$T_{2n} = \tfrac{1}{2}h(y_0 + 2y_1 + 2y_2 + \cdots + 2y_{2n-1} + y_{2n})$$

$$T_n = \tfrac{1}{2}(2h)(y_0 + 2y_2 + \cdots + 2y_{2n-2} + y_{2n})$$

where $h = (b - a)/(2n)$.

(5.13) Write a program to implement Simpson's rule for a discrete data set, based on formula (5.57), which uses only one data point in every p.

In the table below are data in non-dimensional units which relate velocity $f'(\eta)$ to distance η in a fluid boundary layer. Using steps $h = 2.4, 1.2, 0.6$, respectively, and replacing ∞ by 9.6, calculate the integrals

$$A = \int_0^\infty (1 - f'(\eta))\,d\eta \quad \text{and} \quad B = \int_0^\infty f'(\eta) \cdot (1 - f'(\eta))\,d\eta.$$

(These integrals, when multipled by $\sqrt{(vx/u_x)}$, measure the losses of flow rate and momentum, where v = kinematic velocity, x = distance from boundary leading edge, u_x = free stream velocity.)

η	0	0.6	1.2	1.8	2.4	3.0	3.6
$f'(\eta)$	0	0.1989	0.3938	0.5748	0.7290	0.8460	0.9233
η	4.2	4.8	5.4	6.0	6.6	7.2	7.8
$f'(\eta)$	0.9670	0.9878	0.9962	0.9990	0.9998	1.0000	1.0000
η	8.4	9.0	9.6				
$f'(\eta)$	1.0000	1.0000	1.0000				

(5.14) Calculate $\int_{0.6}^{1.4} \log_e x\,dx$ by the Romberg algorithm, based on trapezium rules with $2, 4, \ldots, 32$ steps.

(5.15) Calculate $\int_{1.0}^{2.0} y(x)\,dx$ as accurately as you can for the data of Problem 6, by using the forward difference formula (5.59). Derive the formula (5.59) from (5.52).

(5.16) Write a program for repeated indefinite integration, similar to Program 5.10, but based instead on the trapezium rules (5.63). Using the data of the Sample Run of Program 5.10, compare the effectiveness of the new program with that of Program 5.10.

(5.17) Below are 35 values $(y_0, y_1, \ldots y_{34})$ of the acceleration in m/sec at the end of a vibrating cantilever beam at times t in intervals of 7.8125×10^{-5} seconds, starting from $t = t_0 = 0$. Use Program 5.10 (modified Simpson's rule) to tabulate 35 corresponding values of (i) velocity in mm/sec, (ii) displacement in mm, given that $z_0 = w_0 = 0$. Check: $w_{34} \simeq -0.25$ mm.

y_0 to y_9:

0	-1	3	5	6	4	-5	-22	-46	-72

y_{10} to y_{19}:

-95	-104	-97	-73	-38	1	33	50	47	22

$$y_{20} \text{ to } y_{29}:$$

| −21 | −78 | −146 | −226 | −321 | −435 | −559 | −662 | −698 | −622 |

$$y_{30} \text{ to } y_{34}:$$

| −427 | −159 | 96 | 255 | 282 |

Index

A posteriori (error bound), 74–75, 91
A priori (error bound), 64, 74
Absolute error, 18, 23–24, 35, 109
Acceleration, 131, 135–137
Accumulated error, 124
  Rounding error, 30–31
Accumulator overflow, 86
Accuracy
  Absolute, 19, 23–24, 35, 109
  Of calculations, 2, 19, 21–24, 28, 34,
    61, 75, 78, 117, 119, 123,
    128–129, 134.
  Relative,19, 23–24, 35, 58, 69, 80,
    92–93
Aitken acceleration
  (∇^2 method), 87–88, 91–93
Algebra, 3
  Fundamental theorem, of 82
ALGOL, 1, 5
Analytical techniques, 15–16
Approximation, 28
  Continuous methods, 95–96
  Polynomial and spline, 95–96
Area, *see* integration
Arithmetic
  Fixed-point, 19, 21–23
  Floating-point, 19, 21–23
  Operations, 3, 18, 20–23, 29, 30, 35,
    95
  Unit, 30

Backward difference 88, 103–114,
    116–118, 134–135
Base ten, 20
Base two, 20
BASIC
  Computer programs, 1–13
  Disadvantages of, 1
  Elements of 2–13
  Enhancements of, 12
  Expressions, 4

Function definitions (DEF), 10, 13,
    40–41, 45, 66, 77, 80, 124–125,
    127, 130
Function subroutines, 80
Loops (FOR, STEP), 7–8, 12, 54–56
Main programs, 13
Matrix routines, 10–11, 56
TAB printing, 13
BASIC statements
  Assignment, 2, 4–5, 12, 44
  Conditional, 2, 6–7, 12
  DATA, 5–6, 37–38
  DIM, 2, 8–9, 11, 13
  END, 7, 13
  GOSUB, 9–10, 13
  INPUT, 2, 5–6, 13, 37–38
  MARGIN, 110, 112
  NEXT, 7–8
  PRINT, 2, 6, 13
  READ, 2, 5–6, 13, 38
  REM, 2, 9, 13
  RETURN, 9, 13
  STOP, 7, 13
Batch programs, 37–38
Bernoulli's method, 82–88, 93
Binary, 19–20, 30, 35
Binomial expansion, 114
Bisection method, 62–66, 78, 88, 90,
    92
Boundary layer, 136
Boundary leading edge, 136
Brackets in BASIC, 4
Branching (multiple), 10

Calculus, elementary, 16
Cantilever beam, 90, 136
Central difference, 103–112, 117–122,
    125–128, 134–135
COBOL, 1
Collocation, 95–101, 113, 134–135
Combined algorithms, 78

139